IN CONVERSATION

Samuel Wells
and Stanley Hauerwas

Facilitated by Maureen Knudsen Langdoc

CHURCH
PUBLISHING
INCORPORATED

Church Publishing
19 East 34th Street
New York, NY 10016
www.churchpublishing.org

Cover design by Marc Whitaker, MTWdesign
Typeset by Rose Design

Library of Congress Cataloging-in-Publication Data

A record of this book is available from the Library of Congress.

ISBN-13: 978-1-64065-277-4 (pbk.)
ISBN-13: 978-1-64065-278-1 (ebook)

Contents

Introduction

Stanley Hauerwas (SH): One of the things that Sam and I said to one another in preparation for this conversation is we need to try to go beyond our stump speeches. You know, speeches like my claim that "Modernity names the time when you produce people who believe they should have no story except the story they choose when they had no story." We should want this exercise to force us to say things we didn't know that we thought. You think you've heard any of that?

Maureen Knudsen Langdoc (MKL): I do. The conversation we had about people wishing you would have written more about race, that's something I've wondered about and didn't know your response to until today. And the exchange you and Sam had about human sexuality—I didn't even know we'd talk about that. But it was interesting for me to watch you two ask questions of each other, to push one another to consider the implications of following a particular logic. That seems like a natural conversation between you two, as friends and theologians.

Samuel Wells (SW): That feels some of the strongest stuff, in the sense that we're actually doing it, rather than looking back at it as wondrous things we did some twenty years ago.

MKL: And I think there's been a good bit of conversation about your personal lives, that isn't in print—

SH: I didn't know we would get this personal. It's okay. I just don't know if anyone will want to read about it.

SW: That's what I said to Maureen yesterday!

SH: I mean, why should they give a shit what our personal lives have been like?

MKL: I think the personal life stuff matters, at least to the extent that we've talked about the relationship between thought and action and the formation of character. When I was your student, I appreciated the classroom discussions about Christian ethics, but I also really wanted to know, where does Stanley Hauerwas buy his groceries?

SH: (*laughter*)

MKL: How does this all play out? I think readers will find it interesting to know more about your marriage, what you're afraid of, whose opinion matters to you, what you pray for your children.

Nancy Bryan (NB): It's very much what I want the series to be—that deeper, more personal conversation overlaid with theological topics.

SW: But what you need to know, Nancy, is that for Stanley, the words deeper and more personal don't end up on the same side of the divide. Stanley would regard personal as less deep. (*laughter*) I'm only joking. But trying to get back to twenty years ago before I was in this world, if you will, and if I think about what I'd want to know about Stanley, I think we've covered some of those things. In other words, you have all these convictions and are having these conversations with Aquinas and Aristotle, but how does that map out in the intractable relationships of your life?

SH: I think the order of the book will not necessarily be the order of the discussion.

MKL: Oh, I agree, and our conversation hasn't followed the proposed outline.

SH: I mean, the discussion we're having right now can be a part of it as far as I'm concerned.

MKL: I assumed there would need to be some rearranging.

SH: So where would you put the first discussion, when we talked about theology as conversation and all that?

SW: I think that belongs in the beginning, doesn't it?

MKL: I do.

Conversation One

Theology as Conversation / Constantinian-on-a-Stick /
Claiming the Everyday / The Role of a Theologian

MKL: As part of the *In Conversation* series, our time together is designed around the idea that two theologians who happen to be friends come together to talk about theology, the church, their interests and passions, and readers get the privilege of peering around the corner and listening into this conversation between the two of you. So it seems like a good way to begin is to start by talking about theology as conversation. Would you describe theology as conversation? If so, who are the conversation partners? What's being communicated? Or are there limitations or reasons to resist or qualify describing theology as conversation?

SH: Sam has written about conversation in a very intelligent way, locating conversation as the primary virtue of the university. And what that helps you see is conversations are not just between people who agree but are between people who bring diverse backgrounds and experiences, in which they test out what they think they know by listening to someone else. So listening becomes one of the more important aspects of having a conversation. Whether you have something to say is extremely important, because too often conversation happens between people who think they are already in such agreement that they don't locate how it is that their conversation is really an exercise in group narcissism. So it's very important that conversation is understood as a mode of investigation. All that said, Sam and I have had a conversation for how many years, Sam?

SW: Well, it started in 1991, so twenty-eight years.

SH: And when Sam was Dean of the Chapel, we had many, many, many conversations in which we tested our own perceptions of what was going on, as well as exploring theological issues that we hadn't perhaps known quite how to think through. Sam leaving Duke was one of the most dramatic exits for me. I mean, we still talk constantly, but it's not quite the same in terms of having a face-to-face kind of conversation. The conversation between Sam and myself has been a conversation between friends. And friendship is absolutely constitutive of the conversation, and the conversation is constitutive of friendship.

SW: I guess the way I think about these things is eschatological. The university portrays to the church something that eschatologically the church hopes, expects, and prays to discover in heaven. If you imagine heaven as a place where there's nothing to fix, and there's no deficit to be made up, then whereas popularly people think the biggest issue about heaven is whether you get there, once that issue is taken off the table the real issue is what on earth are you going to do when you're there? And so, part of the work of theology is to describe the gifts that God gives us in such ways that we can begin to imagine how those gifts are inexhaustible. Otherwise heaven is dull, and you don't want to see Stanley when he's bored. So even though I would like to spend a lot of eternity with Stanley, I hope he's not bored because it won't always be a pleasure.

SH: Bernard Shaw said that he preferred hell because at least there would be interesting people there.

SW: In John Milbank and Adrienne Pabst's *The Politics of Virtue*, the most interesting line in the whole book is—I'm sure it came from Milbank—is that liberalism's understanding of the past is that people must have been perpetually bored. That's my favorite line in the whole book.

So conversation is a description of how I engage everything in my experience, from the skills developed in the past, and failures and insights from my own shortcomings, and bring those face-to-face, literally, with another person, or more than one other person, in ways that are like a Van de Graaff generator: they spark and they create problems and they go down side alleyways and so on.

Even the etymology of the word, if you think about the word converse, not understood as a verb, but as *con*-verse   as we pronounce it in England, then you're talking about turning something over and over in your hand, and you don't have to read Julian of Norwich and talk about hazelnuts, but the idea of turning something over and over in your hand to reflect on its multi-significance and its multivalence, is obviously a devotional and spiritual activity. To do that as a group together—to turn something over and over in your hand together is a wonderful thing. And the only thing that really stops you from doing it is time. And that's why it's so important to call this an eschatological practice, because it depicts what human interaction would be like if time were not a problem.

SH: I think that one of the things that's part of conversation is a historization of where you are at the time you are engaged in conversation. Sam has this lovely account of developments within Christianity in relationship to the university. The prologue being when Christianity was in complete control and you didn't know there was an outside. Then chapter one. How do you put that in chapter one?

SW: Well, that was round about the beginning of the twentieth century when the denominations—the judicatories—got the governing bodies and the faculties got the curriculum and they both thought they'd won. And then chapter two as I call it is what we think of as the 1960s, which is now nostalgically looked back to, paradoxically in a way, because that was when universities and the church really mattered. Kent State was at the center of the national attention, Martin Luther King Jr. was a pastor, and in some ways what was being debated was the American constitution. But it was being debated in these kind of places, when academic discourse actually mattered to the whole. Of course, it was really about Vietnam. It was about middle-class kids getting the draft. But people forget that, and they assume it was a sort of heightened awareness in the 1960s.

So basically, what I was saying when I was on campus here was that we were in chapter three. Chapter three is largely characterized by different understandings of the story but is mostly a fight between those who are trying to get back to chapter one and those who are trying to get back to chapter two. But it was really a call to inhabit chapter three. And chapter three, as it might come as no surprise to anyone reading this book, looked surprisingly like Stanley's idea of a university.

And it was very much about the fact that the church only really got to be interesting if it renounced the right to chair the meeting all the time. So the most dramatic example of that I think during my time at Duke was in my final year. It was the tenth anniversary of 9/11, and this is the kind of thing I used to talk to Stanley in the gym about—how shall I handle this situation?

And so, the chapel choir had performed Mozart's "Requiem"— a nice sort of forty-five-minute piece of commemoration, and then four people were going to speak. And so obviously I had a hand in who those four people were going to be, and the four people that spoke were the mayor of Durham, the president of Duke University, myself, and the Muslim chaplain. (People found it bizarre that as the Dean of the Chapel I advocated for hiring a Muslim chaplain because they assumed that the Dean of the Chapel was in chapter one and was clinging onto the privileges of the role, as long as they could be held on to.)

Anyway, we each only had five or seven minutes to speak, but I made my remarks very Christological. I talked about the questions we had about God the Father, in terms of Providence: How could God let this happen? The way we quite clearly saw the work of the Spirit in terms of the firefighters and their work. But as Christians, we could only see it as a crucifying moment. So I got a letter shortly afterwards saying you're not allowed to do that. You broke the rules. And I wrote back with all integrity saying you may not have noticed the rules have changed. Once we've got a Muslim who can talk about it in the light of 9/11, then the Dean of the Chapel doesn't have to talk about all people of goodwill anymore, which in chapter one we thought was identical with Christianity but clearly is significantly different. I get to talk about Christianity for the first time. And actually, it ended up not in a hostile relationship with the correspondent. We became friends, we met up two or three times, and he invited me to speak at his synagogue.

SH: This is an example of what it means for Sam to be the Dean of Duke Chapel. I remember when he was offered the position, I said, I certainly hope you'll take it. It is a preeminent example of a Constantinian church that he would become Dean of Duke Chapel. The office is Constantinian-on-a-Stick. And I said, "Use it." Now that helps, I hope, allay some of the criticism that allegedly I represent a position about Christianity that requires a withdrawal from the world. I'll oftentimes say I wouldn't mind withdrawing but there's no place to withdraw to. You're surrounded.

I think we are now in a situation that makes it possible for Christians to be free for the first time in many years. Because we lost. We're no longer in control. We don't control the conversation. We've got to pick it up wherever it seems to be going. And we can use some of the shards that have been left over from Christendom. And we don't know what the future will look like. But in the meantime, we can have a hell of a lot of fun that the gospel makes possible because we do the odd thing of worshipping Jesus. And that unleashed a conversation that has gone on now for two thousand years because it's such an extraordinary thing to believe that in this Palestinian Jew, God is fully present. And how to think through and live appropriate to that extraordinary set of claims is an ongoing challenge that makes life so unbelievably interesting.

And that is what I find in particular Sam is able to do better than I'm able to do. I mean, that he brought in heaven as part of the conversation is a move that I would find awkward. But he's a pastor, and his job is to do that. I admire it and wish I had the facility to do it. But even though I'm strongly identified with having strong theological convictions and working them out, I find the way that Sam is able to interject into his speech and into his writing, theological claims that do work—his ability to do that—that I find invigorating and humbling. Do you think that's right, Sam?

SW: All I'd add to that is I think I know who I learned that from. And so, I think you're too modest. I guess you could say theology is a conversation between humanity and God but that sounds rather grand. I'd say it starts with a conversation between the Old and the New Testament, and in that sense that conversation is already going on. We're privileged to, just as in worship we enter the worship of God by the angels that's going on all the time, so in theology, we enter a conversation between the Old and the New Testaments, which has been lively for quite a long time before we showed up. And then you've got a conversation that takes place between the scriptures and the early church.

The first book of Stanley's that I read—not the first writing of Stanley's, but the first full book of Stanley's I read years ago—was *The Peaceable Kingdom,* and I vividly remember what he says in *Peaceable Kingdom* that we only have the Jesus that the early church gives us. So that debate about what Jesus really said and that kind of thing that obviously when I was at seminary I got involved with, just as probably everyone at seminary gets involved with. What about the things that Jesus said that aren't recorded in the scriptures? What about the people that feel that Jesus only said two of the eight beatitudes? Are the parts of Paul that probably predated Paul or were written by followers of Paul more or less authoritative? You know, all that sort of debate. I felt that just a few paragraphs Stanley offers in *The Peaceable Kingdom* cut through a lot of that for me at a very significant stage in my own development.

But there is still obviously a debate between the scripture and the early church that goes beyond the period when the scriptures were actually written and brought together as a canon. And then I suppose there is a question which Stanley has raised in a very lively way, which is, does the early church, which one assumes as a coherent, historical entity, constitute a place of authority? Clearly not to the same degree that scripture does, but something to which the church of our age or any age must regard as a touchstone?

And so, when Stanley says the word Constantinian, as he did a few moments ago, the claim of that is that there was a pristine early church before the beginning of the fourth century that had a coherent social ethic and perhaps theology more broadly. I mean this is Pre-Nicaea. It's before the creeds were written down as we know them. But the claim of the Constantinian argument is saying there was a time before that when, I don't think anyone is saying the church got it right, but that around significant things like pacifism most obviously, the church had a more authoritative, authentic, united voice than it has done, in the sense that its compromises are most obviously dated from the fourth century onwards. So that becomes another conversation partner and then there's no end to them.

And of course, we also include a vast range of contemporary ones of which the most obvious today would be other faiths, among whom I don't count Judaism because I don't regard Judaism as another faith. They're our parent. But getting the right range of conversation partners—including people in conversation—is crucial.

SH: I think that Sam's exactly right, that the most decisive decision of the early church was that the canon included what we call the Old Testament. And that meant that Christians cannot avoid trying to respond to the question of how is the God of Israel to be found in Jesus Christ? And that meant that Jews would always make Christians nervous. That's the reason why we were so murderous about the continuing existence of the people of Israel.

And that crucial theological decision meant that Christians could never do without people raising that question, and they're called theologians. I think that one of the interesting things about Christianity is by necessity it produces people called theologians who have to respond to the critical questions raised by, what we regard, as authoritative texts. Not every religious tradition produces theologians. That is an office within the church that is necessarily ready to engage the critical questions that on the whole you'd prefer to avoid. I think that at least if my work has had any strong theme, it is that the commitment to Christ means that fear of raising questions you don't know the answer to must be engaged.

So the truthfulness of Christian speech is not a given. It is an ongoing performance that makes possible ways of life and thought that testify to the joy of what it means to be part of a people who worship this savior. That way of putting it raises then the first question: what does it mean to need a savior? I mean, it's those kind of fundamental questions we oftentimes don't get to because we think it's just a given. What is it about our lives that need saving? Those are the kinds of questions that I think Sam is so good at making present in a way that stops people in their everydayness. Because it's exactly those kinds of questions that show that we've got nothing to fear. And that's hard going for a number of people.

People often think that the position I've tried to develop over the years theologically is such a radical position. But I'm just trying to help us claim the everyday. What does it mean to go through a day in which you don't lie? Now I think Christianity creates such an extraordinary framework for understanding our existence that it makes the everyday possible. And that's what I've tried to do in terms of the kind of writing I've done and the kind of preaching I've done. It's to show how these extraordinary claims about Jesus of Nazareth as Savior make it possible for us to live truthfully with one another. That's a project that has only begun (*laughter*). At least it's the way I see it.

SW: The role of theologian is in a sense a kind of ordained role. What I mean by that is, if you understand that God has given the church everything it needs primarily through baptism and eucharist and prayer and scripture and preaching—the practices of the church—then you need to set people aside to do those very well, if you actually believe those are the things through which God renews the church. You can't just have people showing up saying, "Oh it doesn't really matter what scripture we read," or "I don't know what those long words mean or who all those names are but let's forget about it. Let's get on with evangelism or whatever." You're cutting yourself off from your life source if you don't have people set aside to do those things well and in good order. That's what ordination is as I understand it.

Well, I feel the same way about theology. You need some people set aside and we have a process of doing PhDs and things to fit people for that ministry. And unless you have those people, you're going to run into all the same kinds of dead ends. But that presupposes something that I think is from time to time in question, which is the symbiotic relationship between theologians and the church. And for different reasons and at different times that comes into question. And it's no exaggeration to say that there have been times and places where theologians and the church have despised one another.

SH: Sam, say a bit about why it is that you've been determined not to be an academic, and that your ordination to the priesthood has meant that you stay in a congregation as the pastor. That combination is extremely significant, it seems to me, because it says something about what might be called the academic captivity of theology to the university and that somehow you sensed that that was not your calling.

SW: I want to do this in a way that doesn't suggest that everybody should be like me. I've got tremendous respect for people who are theologians in the way that you have been, but I think I've known for quite a long time that that wasn't the best fit for me and I think it comes from an impatience to see the practical out-workings. I mean, it's not language Stanley or I would ever be comfortable using, words like "applied," but I'm struggling for better language. "Incarnate," I guess would be a more theological word—the incarnations of these insights and convictions about how they address exactly the questions that Stanley just articulated. I mean, it made me very happy to hear Stanley say a moment ago that all of his work has been about how to work out how to spend the day as a Christian.

I chose to pursue conversations around virtue ethics and postliberal theology because they were the ones that most explicitly addressed the question I had as a newly ordained pastor, which was what does a holy life look like for a layperson? I'm still trying to find the answer to that question, but I'm very glad that Stanley became the first principal line of inquiry through which I pursued that question because Stanley, more than anybody else that I'd read at that point and more than anyone else I've read since that point, offered such a thrilling notion of what it meant to be church in a way that transcended and out-narrated any idea that you could have a fulfilled life within your own terms of reference.

And so then the question of why I've never successfully become an academic theologian in a narrow sense of, without needing to do all the other things well two things happened: one is, I never expected my theological training to lead to such extensive opportunities for research, writing, and teaching as they did. I had already been in ordained ministry for ten years, not expecting to do much beyond that in terms of parish ministry, by the time the opportunity to do quite a lot of things beyond that came along. Someone like Tom Wright, for example, it seems to me, is someone who's fundamentally formed by the academy and is also a priest. Whereas I've always thought of myself as the other way around—as someone who is fundamentally formed by priesthood, but is also a theologian, or whatever particular term one wants to use to call that other part. So for me, the noun has been priesthood and the adjective has been theologian.

And then the part beyond that is rather like Stanley, and so Stanley in some way has not been a contrasting companion in this, but a similar companion, and the thing about a similar companion is that they can't critique, so Stanley's not been able to critique the fact that I've also become quite prolific. I've become prolific, I think, because the day-to-day experience of the challenges that ministry has turned up for me have been ones that I have been very eager to unravel. And then the unravelings have developed this twofold character, which is what people seem to enjoy about what I write, which is that it has a very ordinary frame of reference but it has clearly a very vertical engagement with the great theological questions and the tradition and the answers the tradition has brought to those questions. I've really tried to think hard and theologically about the pastoral issues that have raised themselves, whether those are the welfare state or abortion or whatever the question might be. And there aren't a lot of people, rightly or wrongly, doing that. People tend to stay in the silos, and I think the church is the more impoverished for that. But I'm learning all the time from people in both camps, and there are obviously more than two camps, but usually it's thought of as church and academy. I'm trying to remain in close conversation with people in those two areas.

SH: Something that I think is crucial to conversation that we haven't yet talked about is language. Where do you get the language to have a conversation? Language has been so much at the heart of what I've been about, namely Christianity is ongoing training in knowing how to say. We think we already know how to say what needs to be said, but theologically the kind of work that I've tried to do, and I think Sam's trying to do, is to show how the statement that Jesus is Lord is going to transform everything that you have to say. And it sounds simple, but it's damn difficult to get it right. Because Sam's reflection earlier about why a word like "applied" is not a good word for us sounds simple, but it's very important because if you have to ask how your belief is to be applied, then you've got an indication that what you believe is an ideology not a language that's doing work.

And conversations are a constant testing of how we say what we say because the interlocutor always has the right to say, "I didn't get that," or "I don't understand what you're saying." And then you discover that you're not sure you understand what you're saying, in terms of the kind of language that you're using. Because language goes dead. It goes dead when we get so used to it, it doesn't make us think any longer what it is we're saying. And so theology understood as conversation is theology that can never shut down the next question. And I think one of the books that

Sam has done that I just think is extraordinary is a collection of his eucharistic prayers. What's the name of that book, Sam?

SW: In America, it's called *Eucharistic Prayers*. [The UK title is *Joining the Angels' Song*.]

SH: (*laughter*) Well, there you are. I think that they are extraordinary and moving and that it's where Sam does some of his very best work with language. It's good work because he's not afraid of saying extraordinary things about who we are before God. Do you agree with that, Sam?

SW: Well, I'm glad you like the book. That's certainly exactly what I'm trying to do with the book, recognizing how the language of prayer helpfully shapes and expresses theological insight and inquiry. At Duke Chapel, I realized that people commented almost as much about the prayers that I led on the Sundays when I wasn't preaching as they did about the sermon that I preached on the Sunday that I was. And that wasn't just people with a shorter concentration span. It was also recognizing that a lot of people come to church to pray, not necessarily to hear the sermon, even at Duke Chapel.

And the way that I was leading prayers was what Stanley and others like Lindbeck would call a grammar, which ties very much into this conversation about language. And it quickly dawned on me that this wasn't something that enough people were writing about so I ended up doing a book called *Shaping the Prayers of the People* with Abby Kocher, and then she also worked with me on the eucharistic prayers, which was a much bigger project. Nancy Ferree-Clark was the first person that persuaded me to start writing eucharistic prayers for the chapel, which I had strong resistance to doing because Anglicans don't do that.

SH: That was my first reaction. I thought, you can't do that.

SW: Well, I thought you can't but that was the joy of being at an interdenominational place where actually the only person that told me what to do was the president of the university, who actually wasn't troubled by me writing eucharistic prayers, strangely. He had other things on his mind like raising vast amounts of money for the Duke campaign, and so on.

And so we created a book that engaged with the readings of the day in the Revised Common Lectionary, but again a lot of that is grammar in the sense of working out quite basic things that Christians don't talk enough about—like, can we talk directly to God the Father or is it only because of Christ? And is Christ present here with us, or is it the Holy Spirit that makes Christ present and therefore is it always through the Spirit that we appeal to Christ to make our petition to the Father? And if that's the case, that has to shape the way we speak and obviously the way we speak becomes the way we think.

I've also been involved with the Liturgical Commission in the Church of England the last few years and one of the issues that I've raised because I find it so significant is if Christians believe that the Lord's Prayer, for example, shows us almost everything we need about prayer—most obviously that "give us" is about the present and "forgive us" is about the past and "deliver us" is about the future—and if increasing numbers of Christians are finding it difficult to pray a prayer that begins "Our Father," for both sociological and theological reasons, do we have a serious problem? And if so, how do we theologically think about what presents as a liturgical problem but is really a huge theological problem?

SH: I want to call attention to that quick exegesis of the Lord's Prayer. Now that's the kind of thing that Sam can do that I envy. I mean that typology of how the Lord's Prayer is at once about the past, future, and present. I don't use the word very often, but that is just a brilliant quick account that you can easily miss how extraordinary it is that prayer offers that kind of theological moves. When I wrote the commentary on the Gospel of Matthew, I wished I had known that typology. Though I did argue that the Lord's Prayer has within it the whole gospel. But how those categories help illumine how the prayer reaches out to everything else that we believe. I always worry about the word *believe* because it's so rationalistic but it's a placeholder I suppose in a statement like, the Lord's Prayer reaches out to everything we believe. I prefer to say reaches out to everything that we are or have been made.

SW: I think you're okay with *believe* until it becomes the word *belief*, and then it becomes quite problematic.

SH: Belief. Right.

SW: Because it seems arbitrary.

SH: Right. I mean that's an instance of the kind of rethinking theologically that I think some of us have represented, namely, it doesn't occur to most Christians to think that the word *belief* might be a problem exactly because they assume that Christianity represents twenty-six improbable things that you believe before breakfast. Therefore, to raise questions about belief is to direct attention to the significance of what we do when we pray the Lord's Prayer, or what it is we do when we receive the body and blood of Christ.

Conversation Two

Saying Too Much / Against the Grain of Christian Culture / Eschatology / Prayer

MKL: Stanley, you've said that one of the habits necessary for a theologian is humility—not to say too much. Can either of you think of a time when you said too much?

SH: I can't remember any setting where I thought I said more than I should have. I think what I write is sometimes interpreted as saying more than I said. For example, if you take the commitment to Christological nonviolence that I represent, people think that that means I must know what I'm saying when I use the phrase nonviolence. And therefore, you're a pacifist, which means that you always will know what it is you are to do in violent situations, namely you're to refrain from using violence and so on. For me the claims for Christological nonviolence are promissory notes that when confronted you will have to discover that you may have commitments about nonviolence you hadn't known you had.

Or the accusation that I represent a sectarian position, namely that the church is okay, and the world is going to hell and I don't care—that seems to me to be a misreading of the kind of work that I've tried to do. But it is a misreading that I cannot say cannot be gleaned from what I've tried to say.

MKL: Do you feel at all responsible for the ways people have misappropriated your work or misrepresented it?

SH: Absolutely. I feel the responsibility for it. So you've got to do it again: repetition becomes part and parcel of being responsible for what you've done. But the repetition is hard because it can become so boring. I mean, in many ways I've said the same thing over and over again, trying to say it differently in a way that makes it free of defensiveness, and therefore able to do work. So writing is a constant discipline to try to say again what you've said but with an openness to the challenge of saying it differently.

One of the things I often say is that: my strength is there's nothing I'm not interested in, my weakness is there's nothing I'm not interested in. And that means that the work is extraordinarily diverse and wide-ranging in engaging many different subjects, all as a way of exploring what are the implications of what I've thought in a way that invites help. I need help. And Sam's been one of the helpers. Without "Sams" you wouldn't know something isn't right. You've got to write in a way that invites other people to take up the work in ways that you haven't thought about. So, I can't remember when I've said more than I should. But that interpretive work from other people does sometimes take on readings that I hadn't anticipated.

MKL: Sam, is there a time you said too much?

SW: I think the part that I twinge about when you ask that question is I published the remarks that I made the weekend after the Lacrosse story broke here. And actually, if you look at them there's nothing wrong with them. So in that sense, I don't feel bad about them. However, you can never look at things in isolation. At the time on the campus and in the wider discourse, it looked terrible for the players, the way the district attorney had portrayed the case, and obviously it was his case to portray. All the early bits of news that came out corroborated what was later described by bloggers and others as a rush to judgment. And it can happen in a community with a lot of people watching and not necessarily that many people in the inside of a story. But circumstantially it looked like they'd done it. And so it's perfectly understandable that some people in the immediate aftermath and since have seen my remarks that day as being part of that rush to judgment. I think if you look at them coldly now, I didn't do the kind of moves that a number of faculty did, in terms of what I guess in the light of the language we've used earlier, would be to do a rush into chapter two and see this as a race and gender issue.

What I tried to do is say this is about conversation, and things that have been alleged are clearly not about that. And so in that sense then they're not what this university is about. Looking back, it was obviously right to address it as a pastor. I tried to make the actions speak as loud as words. So I didn't use the pulpit. I didn't use a text. I tried to speak from the heart, as it were, although obviously I thought about my remarks quite carefully. Of course in the light of how the case turned out and the fact that the students were exonerated and the district attorney clearly had all the information that would have exonerated the students in his hands very early in the story, and for reasons I still don't understand, didn't make the information public, I do wince a bit thinking that I was amongst those people whose actions made things harder for the indicted individuals and their families because they didn't do things that they were accused of doing and they should never have had their lives so significantly damaged by a widespread assumption that they did. It's not so much what I actually did say, it's whether I could have found something to say that showed more even-handed compassion for everybody involved without saying nothing.

MKL: To nuance the question a bit, Stanley, as you reflect back upon your work, is there anything about which you wish you would have said *more*? Or a silence you wish you would have broken?

SH: Well recently there's been criticisms of me for not saying more about the race issue. I hate that phrase, "the race issue." I mean, the challenge of race is deeper than what it means to be an "issue." The first thing I ever wrote was a piece when I was teaching at Augustana College in Rock Island, Illinois, in the *Augustana Observer*, which I think was the name of the student newspaper. I wrote a piece called "An Ethical Appraisal of Black Power." I did so to counter the claim by Christians that Black Power was another form of reverse racism represented by the Black Panthers. I defended Black Power as the rightful attempt of African Americans to secure their existence in a way that was not using white guilt. African Americans were discovering you cannot trust white liberal guilt because white guilt will kill you. And therefore, I gave it a more or less Niebuhrian reading of, this is a way of claiming power that makes a good deal of sense. And when I taught the core course in Christian ethics here, race was always a very important ingredient that I dealt with, but I didn't write more about it.

It's hard to go back to the 1960s. It was very difficult for white people to write about race because it was like we want to jump onto this bandwagon to ensure our moral worth and you ought to be happy we're on the bandwagon. And it was a way of saying African Americans have something to say in ways that some of us ought to keep our mouths shut. That was part of the kind of thinking of the time. I suppose looking back on it, I wish I had said more. I'm not sure what I would have said, but . . . .

MKL: You answered my next question. That's what I was just going to ask you.

SH: I think I might should have said more about the rise of feminism. I always said in a lecture, the African American movement raises the most determinative moral issues before this society. Feminism raises the most determinative ontological issues, which I still believe in terms of what Sam was suggesting: how seriously do you take sexual differentiation? And how do you understand what the differentiation should look like? I might should have said more about that. But I wrote a good deal early on about the family and about sexual matters that I don't think anyone goes back to look at anymore. But I think they're still pretty good. But I probably should have continued to say more about that.

SW: A bit like Stanley, I think people have sometimes interpreted things I've said to mean what I didn't really mean. To give an example of that, the textbook on Christian ethics that I did first of all with Ben Quash and more laterally with Rebekah Eklund in the second edition makes it fairly explicit that you can't get an ethic of divorce out of the New Testament. So I've had people say, but you're so negative about divorce, to which I've said, obviously divorce is a tragedy when it happens but in saying you can't get an ethic of divorce out of the New Testament, I'm not being negative about divorce. I'm just saying as an exegete that's just a fact. There may be other grounds, as there are on lots of things where on extra-scriptural grounds something seems necessary or even essential. And possibly even good.

And that clearly has bearing on the debate about sexuality, where now people sometimes talk as if the fact that you can't get a clear ethic of faithful, lifelong gay relationships out of the New Testament means that it's clearly something the church shouldn't embrace and endorse. But those people are often the same people that condone and encourage further marriage after divorce, even when on the same grounds if they were being consistent, they wouldn't.

For those who like to divide the world into two kinds of people, in this case liberals and conservatives, I don't fit neatly into one of those groups. Because in very broad terms my theology is orthodox. And my ethics, on the kind of rather narrow range of issues that people seem to make judgments about, some people see as progressive. But the area that I get asked to speak into increasingly and that I possibly should have taken more responsibility for and done more intentionally, is the area of how somebody who thinks about theology in the way that I do comes out on some of these issues in a different place. For those who identify orthodox with conservative, they would assume that I would take conservative lines on certain issues that I don't take.

MKL: Such as?

SW: Well, most obviously, sexuality. And so, for example, when I gave the annual lecture for the organization in the UK called Inclusive Church, a lot of what I was suggesting politely was that I did believe that it would win the debate on these issues in the course of time, but I think it needed to change significantly some of the premises on which it was arguing. Otherwise, its victory (if one uses such a word) would come at a damaging cost. Some people don't understand that, because they want to say, "Well, are you a goody or a baddy?"—but the nuanced theological argumentation that goes into constructing those positions is really important for me.

SH: One of the things that I'm good at and that I think Sam's good at is reframing. We rarely will respond to a challenge on its own terms. And Sam's example just then that you can't get divorce in the New Testament—you can't get marriage in the New Testament. The very idea that the New Testament is pro-family is a very difficult position to show within the text, and therefore questions of marriage and divorce have to be reframed by the fundamental presumption that Christ has brought a new age in which people are not obligated to be married. And that singleness, therefore, is probably the first way of life for Christians, which is a reminder that the Christian suspicion of marriage isn't because sex is a problem. Sex is always a problem. That's why it's always interesting. But what is going on with the church's concern about singleness is not about sex but about why it is that the church is characterized first and foremost by witness and conversion of the outsider, rather than the biological ascription of children.

SW: When I had the privilege of teaching the core course on Christian Ethics, I thought I would take the opportunity to ask the class a question to which I thought I knew their answer. And the question was something along the lines of, "Do you think Jesus was seeking to create an order for society that enabled people to live their regular lives or was he providing such a challenge to society that it would be almost impossible for a follower of his to ever live a normal life?"

And my memory of the vote was almost two-thirds in favor of the first, which I found devastating because I thought even here at Duke Divinity School, the promised land, we were working with an assumption of what you might call the Life Application Bible. That's to say, Jesus came in order to underwrite a bourgeois, suburban, American existence and that was what made the incarnation so valuable, which is a conviction that underlies the success of the megachurch movement in the United States it seems to me, where the Bible is useful and significant to the extent that it helps you with the more challenging parts of your life and leaves the cosmic order more or less unchanged. That's never been my assumption. It didn't take Stanley to disrupt that.

That was part of what I recognized in Stanley's writing when I first read it as a seminarian that I really related to, but it still points out for me that again as the kind of theologians that Stanley and I aspire to be, you're preaching against the grain of Christian culture (to use a kind of antagonistic language I don't usually use), that is always inclined to instrumentalize Jesus, the scriptures, and God in God's entirety, for the purpose of making our life more straightforward and achieving our goals. And in that sense, if people find Stanley abrasive, it's not the Texan stuff and it's not the colorful language he sometimes uses, it's the fact that he will not go along with that, which is what the church, certainly in this age and possibly in every age, wants to believe.

SH: How do you see what you just said as commensurate with our earlier claims about the radical character of the gospel making the everyday possible?

SW: That's a great question. Well, at the risk of being pious, I would say—

SH: That's a big risk to take.

SW: Yes, for Stanley, that's almost too big a risk to take on. To go back to what I was saying about the Lord's Prayer, if you believe that Christ through the forgiveness of sins has healed the past and through the gift of eternal life has turned the future from a threat to a gift, then you can for the first and only time live in the present because if you're without those two gifts, you are imprisoned by the past and you are made wholly anxious by the future, and therefore you are not actually living.

And so, as some of Stanley's essays written in the 1980s about the gift of time and timeful activities and laying brick and so on are articulating, those activities, in a sort of George Herbert sense, are undertaken in the spirit that you are looking through the window to eternity. They are profoundly faithful activities because they inhabit the kind of life that is only possible if you're not haunted by the bitterness and anger and guilt from the past and the fear and anxiety about the future.

SH: I suppose I would say something like what it means to live in the everyday is to learn to live where you are. That's the phrase I think Rowan Williams uses.

SW: Yeah, and it goes back to the sort of idea of living on the square yard that you've been given. There's a desert fathers' line, which I'm sure I first read in Rowan's book on the desert fathers, about living in your cell and your cell will teach you everything. Occupy the square yard kind of philosophy.

SH: Christianity tempts us to think in a utopian fashion in assuming that if we can't make the kingdom present, something's gone wrong. And as MacIntyre argues in *Three Rival Versions of Moral Enquiry*, there's a place for utopian thinking exactly to create imaginative alternatives for where we are, nonetheless it's the case that you have to deal with the world in which you live.

SW: Well, it seems silly when Stanley's written sixty books or whatever and there's only probably Will Willimon who's ever written more books than Stanley (almost as many as in the Bible) to suggest that Stanley could have said more about something, but [I think he could have written more about] the difference between teleology and eschatology.

So when you say, Stanley, and I think you're absolutely right, that we feel bad if the kingdom isn't breaking in, that's because we are captivated by a teleology mindset that, as a hymn I sang in primary school puts it, "Let There Be Peace On Earth and Let It Begin with Me." That our instrumentality brings the kingdom, and that's a teleological point of view because you want people to be acting towards the final cause of the kingdom, and therefore, they obviously want to see some results of their actions and if they're not, that suggests they're either being unfaithful or fallible or God is not working through them. Whereas if you have an eschatological view, we don't bring the kingdom, God brings the kingdom to us. And so, in that sense as Stanley puts it, whether we see signs of the kingdom is not to a significant degree a sign of the faithfulness of our life. Our life is to model the kingdom that we believe when Christ comes again God will bring.

MKL: What might that look like for a theologian?

SW: I mean this is an easy one in a way, but I remember when Stanley and I were doing our first work on the *Blackwell Companion* in December 2001, the theological world in America was like the rest of America, consumed with 9/11 grief, and Stanley was inevitably asked to make contributions to one or two journals and one or two public settings about this. But what he didn't do was make that a pretext for a whole new book or hang on that hook some version of either a sort of huge I told you so, which some people did, or even more worrying, which I remember we talked a lot about during that time, we've got to suspend our convictions because of what this drastic situation calls for. That seems to me another kind of modeling of the everyday that places it in an eschatological context. Pretty much what Stanley was doing at the end of 2001 was saying, actually the important things in life haven't changed. 9/11 didn't change everything and it's important for Christians not to succumb to the language of everything has changed after 9/11, which was almost universal in the culture of the time.

SH: Yeah, my line was, September the 11th doesn't determine the meaning of history. 33 AD determines the meaning of history.

SW: And that's the same response as you say to the person that says, "When were you saved?" Because the answer is 33 AD, or whatever one takes that to signify, rather than the day I came to my senses, to use a prodigal son sort of term. And that is the same affirmation that I'm trying to make, in terms of talking about the past and the future being the benefits of Christ's passion, as Calvin would put it, that make it possible to live today. So every act of doing the ordinary thing is kind of like Jeremiah buying the field at Anathoth. It's a prophetic sign that actually it's business as usual in the kingdom of God.

SH: I do, by the way, have a discussion of teleology and eschatology. I think it's in *Sanctify Them in the Truth*.

SW: Oh, okay. The book that once brought you royalties of forty-three cents?

SH: Fifty-six cents. (*laughter*) And it's one of those places that I try to do very basic theological displays that no one notices, but I argue that—

SW: Or, in fact I notice and later claim as mine. (*laughter*)

SH: Right. But teleology has an inevitability to it, that there is an intelligence in an organism itself which cannot be frustrated.

SW: Ah, the arc of history tends towards justice.

SH: Right. Therefore, teleological accounts can never be understood as gift. Gift can't work because necessity is always there, whereas to see the world eschatologically is to see the world determined fundamentally by God's ongoing gift. And therefore there's not a necessity to eschatological accounts because it is God's ongoing care of the world through providence. Now those kinds of claims just don't work in the kind of world in which we find ourselves—

SW: Some of it is unpublished but I think I sent to both of you the pieces I did about the trip I made to Auschwitz. It was only in articulating what the theological problem with Auschwitz was that I managed to articulate for myself for the first time that actually all intercession is calling on God to give us what will finally be eschatologically given and revealed now. It's all asking for an advance.

This is why I get so personally wound up on theological grounds, as opposed to taste or style, about the intercession that says, "Lord help us to bring justice, help us to know how to witness in the face of our new political leader and to develop forms of resistance" and this kind of thing, because that isn't asking for an advance on an eschatological gift. It's assuming exactly the flaw that Stanley pointed out in teleology that by a mixture of inevitability and our own agency, the kingdom will come.

SH: There's a grammar associated with those prayers. It's called the grammar of *just*. Dear Lord, we just. And that grammar of just says we know you're more powerful than we are but we just want you to do this because we've been basically okay, and so we're not asking you to do anything that is beyond reason, so, *just* do this. Now many of the people that use that grammar are poor. So

I worry about making that kind of criticism sometimes, exactly because they are trying to express a great agony. And, so when Joel Osteen does it in Houston, I want to be able to jump all over it. But when you hear it—

SW: Yeah, and it's a bizarre thing for a pastor to be complaining that people pray. And you've obviously got to find the right time and place to do that in the context of affirmation and so on, but since it is possibly the most visible way in which the church displays its core convictions about God's action in the world, it does seem to be something we should be addressing.

SH: You have to say that the Book of Common Prayer really still remains one of the great resources.

SW: Ah, when you say that do you mean what the Americans mean by that, which is the Book of Common Prayer composed in 1979 or which British people mean, which was composed in 1662?

SH: Right. I mean 62. But the American Prayer Book still is close enough to 62 that the prayers, I think, are quite remarkable.

SW: There are some wonderful phrases from traditional prayers. I mean, the one that comes to mind is the post-communion prayer: *Send us out in the power of your Spirit to live and work to your praise and glory*, which is just beautifully, theologically framed. And you would be fine with somebody praying that at the end of any intercessory prayer. However, what I've experienced in the Episcopal Church is because there is an understandable and appropriate anxiety that these prayers haven't connected sufficiently with the congregation's circumstances and the world's circumstances, people's ways of bridging that gap are unsatisfactory.

SH: My favorite phrase is the prayer given for someone who is sick. They pray for healing and so on, but then they pray, "If I am to do nothing, let me do it gallantly."

Conversation Three

Speaking for God / Being a Cruddy Christian / Other Faiths /
The Devil's Father / A Disrupting Ethic

MKL: Sam, in *Face to Face* you tell fellow clergy that if you've discovered what it means to speak *to* God and to speak *for* God, you may be ready to speak with your people. Can you think of a time when you spoke *for* God outside the context of Sunday liturgy? And Stanley, in your work, do you ever assume you are speaking for God?

SW: The Sunday after the Brexit vote, I did do a kind of a word to the congregation before the service which was carefully, rhetorically shaped and basically said, somewhat to the surprise and the consternation of the community like St. Martin's which is made up of people on the staff of twenty-five different nationalities and the congregation even more diverse than that, we seem to be coming into a time in our country where there is at best anxiety, and at worst hostility, to the notion of a truly diverse people in this country to represent who we are in the future, and that the future of this country isn't necessarily going to look like or speak like this country has spoken in the past. And there are a lot of people who are trying to do everything they can to resist that but those of us who lead St. Martin's, and I'm the leader of them, are basically saying that if this country becomes a place that's hostile to the outsider, if this country becomes a place that's resistant to diversity, and I had a litany, it will still be found here.

And some people loved that. But I got correspondence from people in the congregation who had voted to leave and who felt that I was portraying them as racists and a whole bunch of other bad things. And they were very cross. My response to them was, "I'm sorry if I gave that impression but I think you need to think seriously about the people you're associating with if you voted to leave for other reasons."

SH: I have to say, that was a Hauerwas moment. I mean, that's very much what I want: people who are trained for the ministry that are able to make those discernments and to say exactly those kinds of things. People bemoaning the loss of the church's membership and status in politics, I mean, I think if we had those kinds of moments we would be interesting enough for people to give us a second chance now.

MKL: Leaner and meaner, I think are your words.

SH: Right. Leaner and meaner.
I never think I speak for God. I try to think and write in a way that I think is commensurate with what God has said throughout scripture and the church's and Judaism's interactions with God. But I have never thought that I could speak for God in x or y circumstances. I oftentimes think that I'm a theologian because I'm such a cruddy Christian. I think Sam has a relationship with God. Paula has a relationship with God that I don't. I'm not pious in any way, and I don't mean piety is the only way of having a relationship with God. It's just that God isn't just there for me. And I take it that that's not a bad thing because it creates the condition that you sure as hell have to think hard on these matters. So I just never think that I have a position that would say I'm sure God is saying this, and that we ought to do this because of that. I feel like I'm very dependent upon people throughout Christian history and who I now live around who may have an immediacy with God that I don't. And I try to say what makes them who they

are. And I guess, I mean, I guess I'm so concerned with not taking God for granted that I have to have a certain distance that forces me to think thoughts that I otherwise wouldn't be able to think. I think in that sense, I mean, I love morning prayer. And the reason I love morning prayer is the psalms. I can identify with "I've been faithful, I've kept the law and the world has beat the shit out of me. But you're God." (*laughter*)

MKL: You two know each other as friends, but I wonder how as a priest, Sam, you would respond to what Stanley just said. Imagine Stanley as your parishioner, telling you that he's a cruddy Christian and doesn't have the sort of immediate relationship with God that you do.

SW: I've always felt Stanley projected onto me, partly through Paula. I mean, anytime Stanley starts a sentence, "You and Paula," I know it's going to be a compliment. (SH: *laughter*) My understanding of God is what abides forever. And so hence when people say I'm not a Christian, I always say, "Don't tell me what you don't believe, I'm interested in what you do believe." And if they say, "Well, I don't believe anything." I always say, "Well I don't believe you." Pun intended. "What do you actually think is of abiding significance and value? Tell me about that."

Christians believe that that thing of abiding significance, or collection of things of abiding significance take a personal form that longs to be in relationship with us. And then, the whole of the flow of Christian convictions come from that central conviction. And obviously the fact that that longing to be in personal relationship took form in Jesus. I mean, I think the scandal of particularity has for me been the biggest apologetic obstacle, mountain to climb. And I think that's partly why I think the work that Stanley has done in *Peaceable Kingdom* around that was so inspiring to me at a time when that was probably as big an issue as it's ever been for me, roundabout 1990.

SH: I think, Sam, what I'm suggesting is I sense in you a formation in the Christian tradition from having sat in your father's mass time after time. That there was a substantive formation through that, that I didn't have.

SW: Yeah, so I think that that brings my father into the thing and I've said to Stanley many times, and reminded him of the only conversation that my father ever had with Stanley. And my father's opening words in that conversation I've never forgotten, which were, "He doesn't get it from me. It's his mother; she was the clever one." Do you remember that?

SH: I do.

SW: And just how sad that made me feel because he had such a low estimation of his own gifts. And also sad that my mother had intellectual gifts which never had an outlet. She was a nurse and then she was ill a lot and came from a generation where there would be no expectation she would put her intelligence to work. But also that my father couldn't express fondness for me without putting himself down, which is something that I'm sure a lot of people can relate to.

And yet the reason why he's relevant in this conversation is that when I came across things I would later recognize as Bultmann's critique of the three-tiered universe or something of the sort, that was so influential in mainline Britain, his response was always, "Oh, well, we've always known all of that." You know, it was very much a sense of, tell me something I didn't already know. And that sense that the call to discipleship (although that wouldn't probably be a phrase that he'd have used) but the call to a kind of sacrificial "follow me" response to Jesus was so basic that as long as you were getting that right, these questions would dovetail behind you in some way just like presumably, you know, the first disciples, still had to wash their clothes and dry them and fold them and iron them or whatever. You see what I mean? The Gospels don't record those details because they're not very interesting. And so, for my father it would have that kind of priority order. Yes, of course they had to find something to eat, but the Gospels don't tell us about that because of course it's not interesting. The only real issue is what is God doing in the world and how are you going to respond to it? Everything else could take its place behind that.

And so, I don't think I've ever lost that clarity of vision. These are great things to talk about after dinner for a while, and pastorally sometimes people want to know why their husband died at fifty-three when a lot of people get to live to eighty-four. You have to have a response when somebody asks you that question. But the only questions that really matter are those two questions. That clarity and intensity I did grow up with, and a sense of hierarchy, and I don't think that has ever changed. And also, a sense of how that means you just go to church. You don't sort of say, can I say the Creed today and is there a line in there about what does very God of very God actually mean? There's a kind of, get over it. Get over yourself. Don't think that these questions are unusual or that you're unusual to be asking them. Why did you ever think this was going to be straightforward without question or doubt? That's all part of it.

SH: I think a lot of what we've been saying depends upon philosophical developments that we haven't made explicit, and that the scandal of particularity is related to it, in the sense that through the reading of Wittgenstein and some other philosophers, Mac-Intyre clearly, what postliberal names (and it's a phrase I'm not very happy with) is the presumption that there is a foundational account of knowledge that Christianity may be an exemplification of, and that's the way you are able to claim it is true in a way that you don't claim about other things. The problem with that is the foundational account becomes more determinative than the crucifixion. I mean, I love Sam's *Hanging by a Thread* book, as a way of reminding us that if you need a theory of truth to know that Christ crucified is the Christ that is resurrected, worship that theory, don't worship Jesus. So one of the things that I think Sam picked up from my work was the ability to do theology without any foundational presuppositions.

And it allows for the strong claims about how Jesus transforms everything. And that has to be displayed constantly, and how then that provides, I mean my way of putting it is, if you could know Christ without a witness you would know it was false. You are only able to know who Jesus is from the lives of others. And that is a condition that established Christianity does not want to put up with because, and what I think a lot of people don't get is, there is a symbiosis between a kind of Christendom church and the presumption that you can give a foundational epistemology for knowing who Jesus is. And that means that the very structure of the way Sam and I understand Christianity will make people nervous who desire certainty. Because hanging by a thread is not certainty.

SW: No, but it's designed to embrace all the anxieties. I quite consciously go through most of the conventional critiques of Christianity in that. We've introduced a tradition at St. Martin's (Sally our new associate vicar for ministry, has introduced), *Ask the Vicar*. So during the announcements at the end of the service, a child, and it always has been a child up to this point and it's partly designed to validate the role of children as thinking beings rather than to be entertained and so on, asks me a question.

SH: How neat.

SW: And they've been great questions: "Who's the father of the devil?"; "Who are God's parents?" And the one last Sunday was, "If Jesus is the one that God sent to be everything for us, how come there are other faiths?" And so I tried to give a succinctly and twelve-year-old focused answer as best I could, which was basically saying in coming as a human being albeit also fully God, God in Christ was made subject to the contingencies (although

I didn't use that word), the misunderstandings and misrepresentations that human relationships are always error to. And our scriptures are, we believe, inspired by the Holy Spirit and yet still subject to some of those misunderstandings and misinterpretations. And so how could we be surprised that what we call other traditions could have so much truth and yet in no case the central truth? And so, the Holy Spirit is perfectly capable of working through those scriptures and those traditions. And yet, we believe that the Holy Spirit is only really comprehensible through understanding the particularity of Christ.

So that answer was my best attempt in like two or three sentences to say we don't, and this is something I think I've probably learned from Stanley, we don't get to be the objective observer. Nobody gets to stand in that place. You can only do so from within a tradition and you can be as respectful as you are capable of being by recognizing that God is God, and it's perfectly possible for Christians to learn things they didn't already know from other traditions. But we can neither so rationalize our tradition that it makes sense in anyone's language nor can we stand outside the tradition and claim to have some privileged perspective.

SH: It's interesting how that latter position presupposes there's got to be something wrong with Islam. There's got to be something wrong with Buddhism. I've spent my whole life trying to figure out Christianity; what do I know about Islam and Buddhism? I mean, I would assume that once you've taken the ecclesial position that we've taken, the question is then I better learn a lot about Islam. Not that I've got to know that it's wrong. Obviously, there are going to be differences, and the differences will matter, but you don't have to kill one another over it. At least as a Christian you can't.

SW: As you both know, a prayer that I go back to over and over again is the prayer: "If I love thee for hope of heaven then deny me heaven, if I love thee for fear of hell then give me hell, but if I love thee for thy self alone then give me thy self alone." And sometimes in public settings I point out that it's a Sufi prayer and sometimes I don't, depending on whether people will then switch off for the next fifty-eight minutes if I've made that disclosure. But in settings where it will be well received, it's just a nice gesture to say possibly the most important prayer for me wasn't a gift of Christianity.

SH: It's just stupid to think that Christians have to find something wrong with other faiths. I mean, a four thousand-year history of Buddhism attracting many extraordinary people . . . there's got to be something right about it! The same is true of Islam. But that doesn't mean, well, you've got your faith, I've got my faith, it's all indifferent. There's nothing that follows from that.

What did you say about the father of the devil?

SW: Well, I'm a good Calvinist, as you know, and I would say that if we believe God is the creator then there is nothing that exists that God has not created. And if you take an orthodox position of the devil, I mean I take the same position as you, which is we don't talk too much about the devil because the devil becomes more interesting than God, but if you take an orthodox view of the devil that the devil is a fallen angel, then the devil has pursued a general flaw, that's to say, to not render his (I assume his, to use traditional language) whole life as an act of worship to God. That's a general flaw because we all make that mistake, to a unique degree. But, like the rest of creation I cannot imagine how it will not all finally be redeemed. Because if you believe in the sovereignty of God, it seems impossible for anyone, even by their own choice, which is by definition not fully informed, to resist the transformation that the kingdom brings.

SH: One of the moves that Sam and I both have seriously considered, and I think probably believe, is that God the Father did not send the Son only because we were sinners but the Son was destined to come whether sin or not.

SW: Yeah, I mean, on a popular level like with the Great Sacred Music program I do every Thursday, I find myself returning to that, particularly when talking about popular pieces of theological music like *Messiah*, which is a postlapsarian composition. Whereas, the supralapsarian position that Stanley's just articulated is obviously fundamental to my theology of *with* because it explains in a way that I cannot understand postlapsarian theology having any language for—why there was a creation in the first place. Other than, there was too much love for God to keep it within the Trinity, and therefore it sort of burst out as creation, which has some problems with Creator/creature distinctions and gets you into some theologically difficult territory. The postlapsarian position is so completely dominated in what you might call problem theology, with addressing the deficit of the Fall, whereas this theology I would see as abundance theology, which is God is always looking for a relationship in spite of any, and made more interesting because of, whatever setbacks and flaws and problems arise on the way.

But it's still a minority [position]. Aquinas was on the other side of the debate, but Barth was clearly on this side. But the theology that I grew up with, certainly that which focuses on the atonement, is all postlapsarian. And I just think that as that plays out pastorally and ethically, and you have to be very careful where you say this publicly, but it instrumentalizes God to be the one who is there fundamentally to fix our problem about sin and eternal life.

SH: I think it's interesting to ask, you've got everything you need at the conception of Jesus. Why do you have the life of Christ?

SW: Do you mean, why do I have, or why do all of us?

SH: All of us. Struggling with that question will give you a way of displaying how it is that the kingdom has come in a way that we're part of it. Because discipleship becomes the form of how you know who Christ is.

SW: I think it took me an awful long time to realize that the kind of Christianity that I have felt called to since teenage days, without at any stage wavering (I haven't been drawn to other kinds is what I mean), is different significantly because it is responding to the ministry of Christ in the sense of the one that says go sell all you have and give to the poor and come and follow me. Not wholly mediated by the death of Christ and its meanings. So it's a calling to follow Christ to the cross rather than to accept what the cross has achieved. And in that sense, it has a fairly clear ethic in a way that it's never been one hundred percent clear to me that if your theology is wholly or almost entirely governed by a particular understanding of the meaning of the death of Christ, which may or may not be accompanied by an understanding of the resurrection, it's not quite clear what the ethic arising from that entails.

I've always assumed it was a disrupting ethic. Whereas if you say our salvation is in the bag and there's only one question left, which is do we accept that, it isn't quite clear what ethic arises from that because the whole of attention is about do I accept that, and so presumably you go to church each Sunday to be absolutely sure that you accept that. I think it's taken me a long time to realize that that's where the parting of the ways happens, and it's about the theological significance of Christ's life as you put it, which is really helpful.

SH: It's interesting, of course that puts you in some tension with the Anglican tradition which always has had a high Christology to underwrite a humanism that leaves Jesus behind.

SW: Yeah, well, there's that interesting part in—

SH: *The Politics of Jesus*—

SW: right, about the Anglican sense of incarnation being a word that simply affirms—

SH: we're human.

SW: Yeah, uncritically affirms that, and I recognize that criticism. I think it's a sharp—

SH: powerful—

SW: but unarguable criticism.

Conversation Four

Becoming Friends / Friendship as Preparation for Dying /
The Shared Project / Saying Goodbye

MKL: Sam, elsewhere you've spoken and written some about the initial experience of discovering Stanley and how transformative that was for you. I want to ask you about that in a slightly different way: what longing did he give words to?

SW: That longing that there was an authentic Christianity that basically believed it all, basically enjoyed the church despite its shortcomings and was fully engaged with the issues of the world, and therefore, was not apologizing for scripture, church history, or the current state of the church. But that didn't mean it wasn't penitent and full of lament about many aspects of those things, but it wasn't embarrassed about the core parts of what we cherish, and yet believed that in order fully to engage the world (not a phrase I particularly like), we will have to be fully the church. And [it] ruthlessly and rigorously looked at alternatives to church, whether those were nation or family, or other things and dismantled them.

And I think also in an unashamed and unabashed way, looked without fear at the alternatives to Christianity (in passing, not as a project on its own), with full confidence that Christianity's answers to the fundamental questions stood up very favorably against any alternatives, and therefore it wasn't a kind of leave us alone we're vulnerable but we've got a tradition in which we want to protect. Neither was it a sort of imperial, we're going to so dominate the control-points of culture that you've got to go along with us even if you don't agree. But an unembarrassed and appropriately assertive engagement that truly saw, as I later came to express it, God has given us everything we need.

SH: I thought it was because I had a sense of humor. (*laughter*)

SW: That helped. (*laughter*) That helped. When we talk about the more personal side of Stanley, the fact that we've never failed to laugh at the same things despite being foreign to one another is in some ways part of the connection. You know, different parts of Stanley's work inspired me in different ways. So reading *Vision and Virtue* was just fascinating. I had read some Iris Murdoch, but he put it in a whole frame, and there are several others. But *Peaceable Kingdom* was a different experience in the sense that it really scratched where I was itching like no theological work I had read.

SH: Let me respond to that. It's a burden. It's a burden to be taken seriously by other people. And yet, that's what you want. But if you get it, you're not sure you want it because it all seems so fragile. There always seems like there's something else you need to know to say what you've said. And so, I get letters quite often that say how much you made a difference in my life. You made it possible for me to be a Christian. You made it possible for me to be a minister. I decided to be committed to nonviolence or something like that. And you suddenly think, *I'm hanging by a thread!* And I want this kind of readership that takes me more seriously than I can take myself since I know my own weaknesses, or at least I think I know some of them.

So it's a very interesting moral business to even write in the way that I've tried to write to want to change people's lives. I mean, I taught the core course in Christian ethics here for 20 years. You think about how silly that is. . . . What are you doing when you teach ethics? As I would tell [students], if you need this course to make your life more ethical, it's too late. You will never get it. So what are you doing when you teach an ethics course? I think you're trying to help, in Barth's phrase, you're trying to help them read a newspaper critically, to see what stories are shaping us and so on.

And you're trying to educate and inform people who allegedly are going into the ministry to know how to talk to churches, to their people, in a way to make intelligible what it is that we Christians think about the nature of what it means to be a good person. So I taught the course, but always with the sense, boy do I know what I'm doing?

I think *The Blackwell Companion to Christian Ethics* was kind of the climax of having taught the course on the basis of liturgy for so long. The very attempt to make ethics intelligible within the liturgical shaping of our lives was the attempt to have Methodists rediscover a more determinative liturgical tradition. It's a burden to have students take you seriously and yet that's part of what we're called to do.

MKL: As I recall, you did say we are supposed to care about the things you care about, right?

SH: That's right. That's right. Very good. (*laughter*) I changed the course and made it part of the decalogue for a while, but I think the liturgical shaping was more determinative for me. Sam, I'm sure you understand about being a burden, don't you?

SW: Oh sure, I mean I run across that through preaching and now through the radio. So after Richard Hays was diagnosed with pancreatic cancer, I did a *Thought for the Day* and Tom Wright called. Straight up. I mean, when he calls, he calls three minutes after the broadcast. He's just waiting around. He said, "You were talking about Richard this morning, weren't you? I recognized it." I had shared about three kinds of prayer: the prayer of incarnation, the prayer of resurrection, and the prayer of transfiguration, and how the prayer of transfiguration was about praying for my friend that this would be a richer time of life and more intense and truer living than he'd ever had before because every moment seemed to matter, because it might be the last conversation you had with people and that this would actually end up being a blessing.

Anyway, I got an email from somebody just two weeks ago saying I became a Christian because of that broadcast and recounted to me in much better detail than I can remember exactly what I said, and then he talked about his life since then and how he's changed his approach to all sorts of things.

Stanley, and another friend of mine, John, write letters like that themselves. Not, you changed my life or whatever. But they write to famous people saying, "I enjoyed your TV program," or "I've read *The Remembrance of Things Past* and I'd like to say, Marcel, that I really like the second book more than the first." Stanley has those sorts of dialogues with extraordinary people. I've never done that. And so, I've never written the email that these people write to me so I don't have a context for how they would choose to do that and how in this case, he would choose to do it three or four years after the broadcast.

I never actually think it's true. I always think that God has done something, and they've attached it to this—

SH: I try to think that. (*laughter*)

MKL: So you never wrote a letter to Stanley?

SW: To say that you changed my life? No. I initially wrote and sent chapters of my dissertation to Stanley and he wrote illegible things in the margins, which I said were very helpful.

SH: (*laughter*)

SW: And then he started sending me things. And then I think the moment we became friends was when I came up for your Gifford lectures and we went for that long walk up the mountain. And you brought terrible shoes, completely inappropriate for the—

SH: joggers—

SW: —really embarrassing shoes for the occasion. And it was just a wonderful walk. It was one of those great walks. It was a beautiful day with a fantastic view. We said some very honest things to each other about some personal things. And I said to Stanley, and to my surprise he sort of said to me, your discernment about my life is authoritative to me. I really want to give you some stuff that is unresolved in my life. And I want you to help us together to think through it theologically, with a sort of intimacy, and a sense that I'm trusting you with some difficult things I don't know how to think about, but I really want to be a Christian in these difficult things. And we've gone on doing that ever since. The difference now twenty years later is I actually almost always know what Stanley thinks before I pick up the phone.

SH: Right.

SH: It's interesting the transition from student and teacher.

SW: I think the difference was technically I was never your student, but also, I was writing about you.

SH: I mean, to move from those inequities of power relationships to friendship is something I deeply cherish. I've directed over seventy-five dissertations and I would like to think that with most of those that that transition has occurred, because dependency isn't good for the person on whom we are dependent.

I just was at the *Ekklesia Project*, and a number of my former graduate students were there, and I was still pretty fragile from a health problem, and one of my former graduate students who I had run thousands of miles with when I was a jogger was helping me out. I was taking the medication that made me dizzy and he was helping me, and I said, "Phil, I'm soon 79, I'm not going to be here that much longer." And he teared up and he said, "I'm not ready to let you go." I mean, that you form those kinds of relations is at once a blessing and yet you don't want—and they're not—but you don't want people dependent. Friendship has to be preparation for the other dying. Your friend cannot want you to leave but at the same time your friend must claim you as one like her who may soon die. That is why death and friendship are so closely interrelated.

■ ■ ■

SW: The walk in the Scottish mountains was a threshold moment, but the other, the more obviously professional threshold moment was when Stanley asked me to co-author *The Blackwell Companion to Christian Ethics* because in a sense that's when I moved from being one of many of these seventy-five-type people to being a key interpreter. So, actually I've never asked you, Stanley, was that something that you just sort of decided or was that something that you thought about for a while?

SH: I just sort of decided.

SW: That's what I thought. (*laughter*) You didn't really think about it.

SH: I just knew you were someone who got it. And we had become friends, and I just thought we could do it. I mean, what I really liked about what you learned from me is you learned it well enough you didn't copy it.

SW: So as Stanley says, I haven't imitated him—in my career as it were, in terms of not being a sort of full professor chair in a prestigious university—but also in terms of the publication and discourse. That's all been different. I haven't read as much as Stanley, so I haven't read these interesting books that he cites—certainly not two eighteen-hundred–page tomes in the last couple of weeks that I can just dip into. I haven't got that facility. And I absolutely never betray any sense that I haven't given the comprehensive definitive answer at the end. There isn't that humility. Most significantly, the occasional essay is just not my mode of discourse.

SH: Sam has a gift for categories and typology that I simply don't have.

SW: And examples is another thing that you don't really do, that I make a big deal of. And lists and things like that.

SH: That's true. Of course, I always criticized the Yale education dominated as it was by H. Richard Niebuhr's *Christ and Culture*, which I always said gave people at Yale the impression that the person with the most inclusive typology at the end wins. And typologies are hidden arguments, so I didn't like that. But Sam's categorizations, like the prelude, chapter 1, chapter 2.

SW: Universal, subversive, ecclesial.

SH: Yes. Those are not really typologies. But they are characterizations that depend on concepts that I don't know where they come from, but they're extraordinarily illuminating. So I'm all for that; I just can't do it. I think it's because I have more of a philosophical background than Sam does and work more with analytic categories in that way. But I just admire how Sam's able to come up with those.

Part of what I think we're indicating is the kind of relationship that we have as friends is already constituted by the kinds of theological commitments we have and that that's not accidental. In Notre Dame in November is the twentieth anniversary of their Center for Ethics and Culture and they've asked me to do one of the keynotes and they want me to do it on friendship with the disabled. And I'm looking forward to that challenge.

There is the friendship between Sam and me in which both of us are filled with agency—but there are other kinds of friendship. One of the things that I've been thinking about is what it means for the mentally disabled to claim you as a friend rather than you claim them as a friend. And what is the relationship between that and God claiming us as friends? Because I believe Aquinas is right that beatitude is our becoming a friend of God. And so the kind of theological work we do is suffused by these kind of concrete relations that are all too human.

SW: Our relationship has always had a shared project. And it was particularly intense during my years [at Duke], the "work-out years" as Stanley has described them. There was this general understanding that we were working on a shared project of what the gospel means in an American university—what institutional forms that takes, what surprising developments could turn out to be beneficial, what were challenges that were helpful, what things needed to be resisted, over-accepted, and so on. And that was the unspoken assumption of every conversation: the project.

And we've gone on having similar conversations, even though the project has changed. My conversations with Stanley have often been about St. Martin's or about the wider sort of goals I've been pursuing in the UK, but it's the same conversation really. It's still about the project, and in that sense we're still colleagues even though we aren't colleagues in the same way as we were as fellow faculty members.

And I don't know if Stanley retires, which is a word one never uses in this company, I think we'll still go on talking in the same way because the assumption is that we're still both conceptualizing the same project. And I think that's different to almost all of my other friendships, where it's taken for granted that we're living in different worlds, but we have a spark in the relationship, which includes things like gratitude or shared memories, where it's just being together that's good or sharing the thing we've always done together. Whereas with Stanley it's almost like we're working on a project together all the time. So we're still in the workshop. We're still in the studio, even if we're three and a half thousand miles away on the phone. That's been there since the very beginning, as Stanley put it, in terms of sharing theological commitments.

SH: One of those things about sharing a project is how much it involves judgments about other people. We're gossips.

SW: Stanley's a gossip. And I play along with it.

SH: I mean, how to get people right. And whether that's really a gesture that shows they really care about something, or it's really just an outworking of their concern that you notice them. I mean, Sam and I do a lot of that kind of thing because we're interested in people and character judgment.

SW: And when you've left such an impression on somebody as Stanley's left on me, inevitably you find yourself saying either out loud or to yourself, "As Stanley would say. . . ." When you've spent as much time together as we have, you hear what the other person would say. And then of course you've got to deal with their judgment, which you can't argue with. And yet sometimes you find yourself in a position where you can't act on that judgment. And of course, there are parts of British culture that Stanley, bless his heart—

SH: —will never get. Cricket.

SW: Right.

SH: But friendship involves, at least the kind of friendship between Sam and myself, involves discovering judgments in common that you didn't know you had but when you discover them, they're very important. And judgments are always about matters that can be other. So there's no necessity to them. So it requires the development of insight. I've just recently been thinking about the importance of insight and where does it come from. Why do some people seem to have it and other people don't? What makes it possible for them to articulate the insight, and in particular it's interesting how insight works about judgments of other people. Because where you think they're really forgiving, in fact, they're manipulative.

Sam's sermons are so compelling because they're filled with insight. I'm pretty sure that insight pulls us into other people's positions in terms of producing agreement in a way that the more philosophical abstract arguments do not. But we tend to concentrate on the more abstract. Where does insight come from?

SW: I mean, it's reflection on experience, isn't it? If I was a practical theologian then I'd call it praxis.

SH: By the way, I don't think you saw the paper on practical theology I did for the Dallas event.

SW: I don't think I did. But I imagine it was full of derogatory comments.

SH: It was completely full of derogatory comments.

SW: (*laughter*) That doesn't surprise me. I would have enjoyed writing a spoof version of that: "I hate the fact that I've been asked to talk about this because it presupposes the idea that theology is impractical—"

SH: Yes.

SW: "—and puts them in contradistinction to one another, which I find to be typical of the malaise of the current academy and church—"

SH: That. And I say it's somewhat ironic that I've been asked to do this because I do not have a reputation for being pastorally sensitive. (*laughter*)

SW: That's right. I missed that line. (*laughter*) Exactly. I'd love to read it.

MKL: As you've been reflecting on the journey of becoming friends and the ways you have an authoritative voice in each other's lives, I'm wondering what it was like for you both when Sam left Duke? Do you recall your conversations about that transition?

SW: I think there was an easy conversation and there was a hard conversation. I hope this isn't speaking out of turn, but I think there was a part of Stanley that wanted me to take up his mantle like Elisha as a very visible proponent of theological ethics at Duke. That was the easy conversation to just say, "Stanley, we're different people. That's not my calling." And Stanley fully respected that. The painful conversation was to say to Stanley, "I'm coming to the conclusion for a mixture of reasons, not least the fact that the then Archbishop had a perspective on things, but also issues like the children's identity and Jo's parents' later life, that Jo and I need to be thinking about going back to England." And that was the painful conversation.

SH: And we both teared up.

SW: That was a really painful set of conversations, particularly as Stanley had been so instrumental in my coming, and we'd had such a close relationship while I was here and that sense of the project that we'd never specifically articulated. (That story where he said, "Use it," was probably the closest that we came to articulating the project.) Those were quite emotional conversations, and I remember the time when I told Stanley I'd said yes to going to St. Martin's. That was hard.

SH: That was hard.

SW: It's probably not an exaggeration to say Stanley's head and his heart were in different places. In his head he got why this was an appropriate thing to do. But with his heart he absolutely didn't get it because we seemed to have developed a degree of conversation that was professional and personal that neither of us had really experienced over time with a friend and colleague before, and I can't imagine replicating.

SH: Part of my head was thinking about the children. Did Sam and Jo want them to be Americans? And I understood that having to decide if they didn't go back about that time, they would be Americans not English. And I quite appreciated the importance of them being English. Now how to understand being English while at the same time thinking the more important thing is being Christian—you had to be Christian the way English are Christian, I suppose. And so I quite understood the necessity of going back in terms of the children. I thought also as a friend of Rowan Williams that it was a good thing that Rowan was asking Sam to come back to do this.

SW: As far as our relationship was concerned, while at every stage I felt Stanley completely understood what I was doing I knew there was some heartbreak there. And it's one of the hardest things in life to know that you're hurting somebody you love but still to feel you need to do it.

SH: Part of the background was how Sam got the job in the first place. I mean, it was a fucking miracle. I had put his name in, but I didn't think he had a chance in hell. And Dick Broadhead interviewed him, and Dick had just terrific judgment in people. I mean, Sam was nobody. He was the rector at Newnham. Dick called me over and he said, "That Sam is something. If I offer him the job, will he take it? And will he keep it?" I said I had told Sam that if he comes he's got to give us seven to ten years. And Dick offered him the job.

SW: Well, actually Dick called me twice. The first time to say *if* I offered you the job—let's possibly imagine—how long would you stay? And we put the phone down. And then a week later he called and offered me the job.

SH: Sam made the chapel the center of campus. It was quite a show.

Conversation Five

Childhood / Loving What Can Be Taken Away /
Praying for Your Children / How Marriage Changes You

MKL: Who was Stanley Hauerwas as a child?

SH: It's interesting that yesterday morning I did my email and then I thought, I'll read *Hannah's Child* and went back and I read about my growing up. Of course, I remember my mother and father very well, and I read that letter I wrote to my grandsons when my mother died, and I thought that captured her very well. And then the sermon I preached at my father's funeral was also, I thought, well done because he was such a gentle man. But what comes through in that chapter is work. I mean, that's what we did. We worked. And I remember just as a very young boy, four or five years old, my mother teaching me how to hoe because we had a big garden and you had to hoe to break up the soil so the plants could grow well. And then being taken out to the job with my father, which was all work. So it was that kind of life that I think instilled habits in me that I've never lost somehow, that you work.

MKL: What was your temperament like as a child?

SH: I'm not sure I know. I think I was hungry for attention. I remember when I went to school that the teacher said my only problem was that I talked all the time. And they put a little sign on my desk that said, "Be Quiet."

SW: Hmm. How's that going?

SH: Right. I learned to disobey it very quickly. I was the only child, and I was just hungry for attention. I don't know why, but that's what I seem to remember. I talk in *Hannah's Child* that I had trouble learning to read.

And my graduate students have long had the thesis that I'm dyslexic because my pronunciation I so oftentimes get was wrong. And I don't know but I taught myself to read by discovering books about baseball, and I just read one book after the other. So I started learning to read and by the end of second or third grade I was reading way above the standard. So reading has always been very much part of my life.

MKL: As we're celebrating your birthday today, do you remember or recall any birthdays as a child? Did your family celebrate birthdays?

SH: I don't remember. We didn't make too much of it, I'm sure. I don't remember, for example, a cake. I don't know my mother's birthday. I remember my father's birthday because it was December 24th, which was always confused with Christmas, of course. But I'm sure we didn't make too much of it. I mean, you're talking hardscrabble life here. You just don't have time for a lot of celebration.

MKL: What did your family have time for?

SH: Church. That was pretty much it. We went to Pleasant Mound Methodist Church. And so you had plenty of time for that. Sundays were taken up with church because you went to service in the morning, but in the afternoon you were involved in some kinds of activities. Every year you had graveyard day, because in Texas, the Texas weather would make the grave dusty and so you would go and clean off the headstones and re-mound the grave. And that was a big event. It left a lasting impression on me that you had graveyard day. It certainly reminded you that you're not going to get out of life alive. (*laughter*) So church was very much part of it in terms of having any extra time.

MKL: You talk a lot in *Hannah's Child* about the Methodism of your youth. Is there a story, or a particular experience, that you could identify that captures the Methodism of your childhood?

SH: Well, there was the emphasis on you had to have the experience of salvation. So the experiential aspect of it is something that I remember. And I didn't like that. Since I never had the experience, I suppose that was part of the motivation behind me dedicating my life to the church at that Sunday night service. I must have been twelve or somewhere in there. That was in the new building that my father had supervised the building of. I remember that more than I remember the white frame of Pleasant Mound Methodist Church. The story that I like and I use in *The Character of Virtue* for Laurie Wells is that about Dad Haggard. This elderly gentleman, and he was in his eighties, would sit on the front pew of this white framed church and when Brother Russell starting to preach, he had a hearing aid that was very large and that he would hold up to try to get as much of the sermon as he could.

And we were always told that we were to love Dad Haggard because Dad Haggard loved all the children of the church. On reflection I can't remember any indication that he loved all the children of the church (*laughter*), but he finally died. And I remember it was a Saturday that the funeral was taking place. It was one of those hot Texas days, and sweat was just running off of you. And Mother and Daddy were sitting at the side part of the church, and I was there, and it suddenly became time for the congregation to view the body. So they got up and we were in line and my father was holding me and I thought, I do not want to see this dead body. Because death was still something that I really didn't want to come to terms with, I think. But when we got up to the casket, Daddy turned me around. I had to see Dad Haggard, and I had never seen him look better! (*laughter*) They had put rouge on him, so he looked better than he had ever looked alive. And they had put a red sash ribbon that kind of had gold tinkles on it with Elmer's glue, and it said, *Eternity Is Now*. Those are the kind of memories that sear into you, that I remember as part and parcel of the general way of life at that time.

MKL: One of the things that I think people find most interesting about your life is the way that you have been in the academy, but still seem to retain the habits of growing up working class. Did you ever feel like your life in the academy distanced you from your family of origin?

SH: Oh, absolutely. Going to college didn't create a kind of alienation between my mother and father and myself but going to Yale Divinity School certainly did. Literally you were being initiated into a way of life that my mother and father could not imagine. The very idea that you spend most your life reading books was of course odd for my mother and father. I don't think they could imagine what it meant to be at Yale and the kind of life that people led that were associated with Yale.

The story of my father and the gun, I think, is the single event that helps name what being at Yale meant in terms of the relationship with my father and mother. That I said, "Someday we are going to have to take these goddamn things away from you people," is a challenge from a world that my father had no idea existed. My mother and father's great gift to me was to let me go on—that metaphor of going on, going on to a way of life that they could not envision. And they knew that. They thought that was okay because it had to do with being Christian. I think that's the way they kind of gave an explanation of it.

MKL: The story of the gun gets at this a bit, but I'm wondering what it means, or has meant to you, to honor your parents in the midst of that sort of alienation.

SH: I think *Hannah's Child* was the attempt to do that. My mother was pathologically afraid of being forgotten, and that was an unfortunate passion of hers as far as I was concerned. But I wanted her to be remembered, that's what that letter to Joel and Kendall was an attempt to do. Sam used a phrase once in our discussions that our lives after all are just a flicker. And our lives are just a flicker. And we will be forgotten. But in the meantime, what a wonderful gift being alive is, and if we try to secure that we will not be forgotten, we will be forgotten all the quicker. So it's my attempt to name, in terms of giving description of my mother and father, to name what good people will look like, who will be forgotten. Just as I will be forgotten.

MKL: Your mom was afraid of being forgotten. What are you afraid of?

SH: That's Cornel West's question. I have a profound fondness for Cornel. What are you afraid of? (*pause*) I'm afraid of disappointing the people for whom my life has mattered. I'm never confident that I am what they think I am. And that is a fear that I'm not sure is appropriate or not, but it's there.

I don't know that I fear it, but I dislike growing old. I wish I knew how better to do it. As someone who has edited and written in a book called *Growing Old in Christ*, which I think is a very good book, I should know better how to do it. But I don't know how to do it well. I thought quite a bit about dying, but I didn't think that much about growing old, and it is a distinct challenge that I wish I knew better how to negotiate. Again, I'm not sure that I fear growing old. It's just that I don't like that.

MKL: That fear of disappointment . . . are there times when that seems to lessen for you? Or times when you forget it?

SH: Yes. I forget it usually when I'm preaching or giving a lecture, and I'm so constituted by what I'm trying to do, it's like you're being taken over by another spirit. And I really believe what I'm saying because it's been a struggle to try to say well what I think needs to be said. So you're consumed by that which you have created, and trying to convince others of. And it's those events that oftentimes create people who are deeply influenced by yourself, and then you're not sure that you want them to be that convinced exactly because you don't want to take responsibility for the position that you've asked them to assume.

That's where I often point out that there is a kind of immorality to the position of nonviolence because to be nonviolent may well mean you will have to watch others suffer for your convictions. Because there may well be a context in which people are being murdered in which because you are nonviolent you cannot rescue those that are being murdered. That's a dramatic position, but I'm ready to take on the most dramatic.

That you may well have to watch people suffer for your convictions, I take it to be an indication of what any serious moral position requires. And we don't know how to say that to one another, or to comprehend it as part of our way of life. I mean, the people that may well have to suffer for your convictions may not even share your convictions. So, it is a deep challenge. I think people committed to just war [theory] have the same. If you're committed to just war, you may well have to watch people suffer for your convictions. Therefore, if that is true, there has to be some very deep reasons for so living, and I take it that the very deep reasons are all Christologically to be articulated.

MKL: This sense of responsibility, towards those who may suffer for your convictions and those who take you seriously, these are folks you may never meet. I wonder what you want for your son and grandchildren? I distinctly remember learning from you that if I'm parenting well, my children probably won't be popular, and their safety shouldn't be my primary concern.

SH: Right.

MKL: What do you want for your grandchildren?

SH: Well, first of all, given Adam's being raised in an extraordinarily tense household, with his mother's mental illness, I regarded it as a great gift that he was confident enough in himself to have children. What a remarkable thing that is. He and Laura, his spouse, have been extraordinary parents and have raised Joel and Kendall in a way that makes them delightful human beings to be around. They've been raised in a church that's UCC, which I always say stands for "Unitarians Considering Christ," so they have conventional Christianity. I hope that may be the occasion to have them grow further into the faith.

How the young are brought within the gambit of what it means to be a Christian in a very serious way I think is very tricky. And I hope for Joel and Kendall that someday they'll have to think, how in the hell do I explain Granddaddy, who spent his life trying to make it possible for Christianity to be reclaimed as an extraordinary adventure? So that's about as much as I have in terms of expectations. From time to time someone says to them, "Do you know anything about Stanley Hauerwas?" And they'll say, "Well yeah, he's Granddaddy." But I hope they may have to be put in a position that someday they may even be embarrassed by that, and then by being embarrassed by that they'll have to know more about it. So that's what I hope for.

MKL: What do you pray for your grandchildren?

SH: I pray that they will find mentors who are more serious than I've been. I had John Score, who was my teacher in college, who made all the difference for me. You just pray that certain people pop up and will give them a way to go on. They are of course children of the middle class, or maybe a little better off than that. One of the things that money does is save us from having to be serious. So you hope that somewhere down the line they're forced into the recognition of the seriousness of life that on the whole we're protected from in certain class levels.

MKL: What do you pray for your two children, Sam?

SW: That God will be with them. That they will know God is with them. And that that will become the defining understanding of their life. That's it.

MKL: How would you describe what you want for them?

SW: I think what I want for them is that they find joy in others, in relationships, and in finding a way of making a contribution to the world that gives them joy, in the making of it and others' joy in the experiencing of it.

MKL: So I'll ask you the same question, who was Sam Wells as a child?

SW: Well, I was very conscious of three stories, I think. Story Number 1 was that my sister and brother had died shortly around the time of birth, and that I was number four and I was a precious gift, hence the name Samuel. I was very aware of that from quite early on. Story Number 2 was that my mother was a refugee, who was a child of a refugee, and that she had tried very hard to eradicate her German accent, and no one was to know. So in that sense, I always had a secret. And I guess there were four stories because the next one that occurs to me is that my father was doing a very important job, and he needed his family's support, and so everything we did was to reflect on his work in a good way. So we mustn't do things that made his work harder. And Story Number 4 was that my father was a clergyman, whose father had been a clergyman, whose father had been a clergyman, but that was not a straightforward life not least because my father had lost his beloved sister when she was thirty and his even more beloved brother when he was forty-two. He was called Martin, which is my middle name (and also happens to be Stanley's middle name, and also the name of the church I now serve). And so, tragedy came with the package.

My mother got very ill when I was five years old, and basically remained ill until she died when I was eighteen. So that was the dominant story which affected almost everything. It's hard to think of anything that it didn't affect. If we went on holiday it was a holiday to make her feel better. She spent two or three hours of the day resting upstairs. I would bring her a cup of tea when I came home from school. And so I think it was also somehow a story my sister inhabited more successfully than I did, because she and my mother were very close and talked about everything, and I think she was really my mother's best friend—even from the age of eight, when my mother was first ill. So there were quite a few minefields is what I'm saying, which I think left me quite timid and anxious.

The other two overarching narratives are, that my father was English as apple pie, third-generation clergy, stable and gentle and trustworthy, reliable and steady, and often overlooked, with a very low sense of his own value. I think largely that came from having been the fourth child in a family where the first and third child were beloved and the second and fourth child were for some reason not. The two that were beloved both died, so he had that sense of survivor guilt, I suppose.

And then my mother being from a Jewish family with this dislocation history and yet, her parents became Christians of a very conservative and almost Brethren-like character whose lives were dedicated to converting Jews to Christianity, which at any time since the second World War has been an extremely unfashionable thing to do. And so that added to the secrecy, really.

No one was allowed to know that my mother was ill. No one was to know about the Jewishness and the refugee story, even though they must have wondered about my mother's accent. There were just all these things we knew about but didn't talk about. So I think I was trying to find my way in the midst of that, constantly aware that I might be doing something wrong—not wrong morally, but just getting it wrong. I didn't like going to school. There was nothing wrong with the school, but I tried to find excuses not to go.

I grew close to my sister particularly during my teenage years. She went away to university when my mother got very ill, and I got much closer to my sister at that point. Finding faith of my own, there was quite a lot of anger. I don't think of myself as an angry person, but I think there was quite a bit of anger because when I read the gospels, they are all about poverty. Apart from a year in Canada where I was born, my father served the same church between Bath and Bristol for thirty years, including three years after my mother died. It was a very middle-class community. So I think that disconnect between what Christianity should be about and what it seemed to be about was really strong through my teenage years, and from about the time my mother got really ill and was dying.

Looking back, I'd say the fact that she was dying was a bigger deal to me than when she died. And the truth is it was a relief when she died, and that took me a long time to kind of forgive myself for acknowledging. I used to have dreams in which she came back to life, and I said it's much easier if you die. And that took me a long time to forgive myself for. But of course, pastorally, it's obviously very helpful for me to have been through an experience like that, to recognize that people can feel things they're ashamed of which are just perfectly understandable if you hear the whole story and help people come to terms with their own fragility and being overwhelmed, which is kind of what I was really.

SH: It's interesting, Sam, church has always been in our life.

SW: Oh yes.

SH: And it has given us a project, continuing to try to figure out what in the hell it's about.

SW: Definitely.

SH: And so it really is that we're Christians because we just find it so unbelievably puzzling that we are. And because it's so intellectually stimulating.

SW: It's the struggle for meaning, isn't it? And that's what I had in church. I think church became one safe place and studies became another. I probably did longer essays than I needed to for my English A-levels and History, and I remember spending Sunday afternoons and evenings in the room we never really used, and that became my safe place. And I've often thought that actually when I write books I'm going back into that period of being sixteen and finding a solace and refuge and sanctuary in writing, to work it all out.

SH: What do you want for Laurie and Stephie in the long run? I heard joy.

SW: I think this is something people have huge diversity about, which is how much agency they believe themselves to have in their children's lives. If you do *Little House on the Prairie*, then every event in life has a moral which enriches your children's character. I've never taken that line. I may be very wrong about these things. I'm not saying this because I think I'm right, I'm just saying this is how I am. It doesn't really occur to me that I'm a role model or a teacher to them. It's certainly my role to give them security and stability in a safe place to grow up and make their own arrangements. But I don't think they need to follow me professionally. I don't think they need to like the things I like.

Oscar Wilde said that selfishness is wanting everybody in the world to be like yourself, which is a classic Oscar Wilde insightful line. And I don't think I do want them to be like me. I want to have enough in common with them so that as time goes on we can share common interests. I'd love to be able to go to the theater with Steph and to watch a sporting match with Laurie, for example, because it would be wonderful to share in those things together. I want them to be able to sort of find their sweet spot and flourish in that way.

I want them to have the experience of friendship, which has been such a huge part of my life, and such a crucial part of my life, I think. I would love them to have a faith that is, as I've said, the touchstone of their life, although what that faith will look like in the next generation is probably quite different. I think from my generation to Stanley's will have much more continuity than from mine to the next generation.

SH: I think that's a very important point. I think in fifty years to say I'm a Christian is going to be a very important declaration because there's not going to be that many Christians around. So you have to then answer the question, well why would you want to do that? So I hope we're moving into a world in which it's impossible to be a Christian without that naming commitments that seem quite odd to the wider society.

SW: That whole story with my mother is still the defining story for me. To invest in relationships that can be taken away from you has been the great quandary of my life. You don't want to be the pastor who preaches about [your own experience] every week, but to the extent that it's helpful for people to know that you know what bereavement feels like and what terminal illness feels like, that sense of how long is this going to go, and will there ever be a normal—it seems that has been helpful to others.

SH: That's interesting. In terms of sermons I never use my own experience. I just have a sense that it's inappropriate.

SW: I started with that, but then I realized that unless you share a degree of your own person, people would feel frustrated and then they would end up making it up. That's particularly for a clergy person in a parish. It's part of how you share yourself.

MKL: Sharing your own experience is different than sharing your family's experience, yes?

SW: Oh yes. I just have a rule that I don't talk about my children or my wife. They just don't appear, with very, very few exceptions. I keep that rule (a) because I don't want my children to grow up hating me for having used them as meat to fatten up my sandwiches, as it were. And (b) I want them to trust that when they tell me their most intimate things, they're not immediately going to be shared with the world—and with the web and everything now, they can reach an awful lot of people and never be gone. But also I don't like the subtle message that you're giving to the listener about your family life.

SH: Right. Right.

SW: Which is usually, I am truly an outstanding and gifted parent and you can never be as talented and loving as me. And to end up with a combination where you told the world you're a talented and loving and uniquely gifted parent *and* your child feels resentful that actually you've used their most intimate or foolish moments as fodder for your own self-advancement is an absolutely catastrophic position to put you and your family in. Why would you do that? So the simplest way is to just draw a line here and say that's not for general consumption. It also takes a little bit of empathy to say, if one of my children were to do a talk at their school and talk about the eccentricities and the rather more embarrassing shortcomings of their father, I would think, please don't do that. So what right do I have to do the same to them?

The only time I really broke that rule was when Stanley did *The Character of Virtue*, which I asked him to do when Laurie was about a month or two old. And recently I told my son that Stanley and I are talking about doing this book, and I said to Laurie, how do you feel about it, giving him a sense of the kind of things the book refers to, which are mostly about him as a baby, or things that wouldn't have lasting significance about his identity and that we weren't disclosing secrets. And he shrugged his shoulders and said it was no big deal to him. So I hope in thirty years' time he still feels it's no big deal, or that it's nice to have.

MKL: Stanley, you did something similar with *Hannah's Child*, yes? You ran the manuscript by Adam and Paula?

SH: I did. Paula read it and she had veto power over anything in it, which she did not exercise. Adam simply could not read it. He just said that to revisit that early life with his mom was just too painful for him to undertake. He may read it sometime later. I don't know. I think he still has not read it. I always give Adam and Laura and the kids my books. I don't expect them to read them. I don't know that what I'm trying to do is commensurate with their everyday life. I mean, I'm an academic. (*laughter*) I'm taking on conversations that not everyone has to have.

MKL: As we're talking about family, I can't help but think of Stanley's rather frequently-quoted phrase about modernity's story, where you say that you always marry the wrong person—that who you are after marriage is not the same person as when you entered into the marriage. I'm interested in hearing from both of you who you think you've become on account of your marriage.

SW: We're getting to quite honest territory now, aren't we? When I got married, I could no longer pretend I was poor. Because I married a person, one of whose parents had been very successful in business. And that made me face up to some significant identity and sort of gospel questions about wealth and poverty, which created some genuine tensions for a while.

Because I was coming to terms with this new identity, and you'd think having more money to spread around would be an unambiguous blessing but I didn't experience it like that. I realized that actually there was something better than that in my universe, and that was having the high moral ground. And I no longer had the high moral ground. So getting used to no longer having the high moral ground, to be able to blame poverty on the rich, that took a while for me to inhabit. I probably said some stupid things, and felt some inappropriate things, as you do when you're getting used to a new identity.

What changed everything was nothing to do with my wife. It was the experience of being in a neighborhood that was given a huge amount of government money and finding myself on a body of people distributing fifty million dollars in a relatively small neighborhood and realizing how difficult it was to make money make things better. And that changed my whole perspective about wealth and poverty. I stopped thinking that poverty was fundamentally about money. And at the same time, I stopped thinking that poverty was fundamentally wealthy people's fault. That didn't mean we don't care about inequality. But I realized there was something about poverty that was more fundamental than simply the having and not having. And that changed how I thought about the money and my wife's family.

SH: I think the big challenge for me is Paula and I are very, very different people. If we've got a problem, I say, "Do this." I don't think it through; you just do this and go ahead and get it done. Paula says, "Wait, we need to stop and think about this; we can't make a decision today." It drives me crazy! So I have slowly learned sometimes not to just charge ahead, and that's hard for me. There's a deliberateness to Paula that I don't have, and I've learned to listen more than I think I ever used to be able to listen, in terms of not making decisions that I probably would make if I could just go ahead and not deliberate about it.

I think one of the things that is crucial to our marriage is Paula's priesthood. I really have nothing but joy at her work at Holy Family, and I think that joins us in a common set of commitments that lets the difference be different. Because in terms of characterological disposition, I'm never going to be as patient as she is. That's certainly been part of the change that marriage has caused in me. Does that fit your perceptions of me, Sam?

SW: Definitely. I would have given a very similar answer on your behalf. I think one of the things to add, something that's less complex, is that Jo and I are constantly surprised that we are each people who regard the word change as almost invariably positive. So . . . invitation to go to America? Okay. We'll go to America. Invitation to go back? Okay, we'll do that. The assumption is that, who knows what lies in the future, but there is a sort of, okay, let's look at that. Some people find change and grief are the same word. I don't think we're like that. I think our reasons for enjoying change are different, but they overlap sufficiently to make for an ability to accommodate and absorb significant changes.

SH: I always sense that Jo is able to deal with the details of change better than you are.

SW: (*laughter*) Sure. I think that would be fair. On both transatlantic moves, I did get to a point where I simply couldn't comprehend what we were going to do with items of furniture or a car. Jo's ability to think through those things far surpasses mine. On both occasions I managed the professional transition and the enculturation of the children, but the sheer logistics of it were daunting.

MKL: You've talked about the importance of having a shared project. Since you and Jo are both ordained clergy, has it also been important to have separate proj—

SW: Yes! (*laughter*) I don't know if she fears working with me more than I fear working with her, but the difference would be quite small. But I think we've always felt we were still doing the same thing. So what our marriage would be like outside church, I have no idea.

SH: Same for me.

SW: I think we do work quite effectively together when it comes to something like cooking a meal for friends. Obviously, it leads to some arguments as it does for every couple because she doesn't always realize that my way of doing things is infinitely superior to hers. That's true in every household in the world. And I think you just have to have some grace around that. You get better at recognizing what triggers the other person's insecurities and frustrations, but you never get perfect at it.

But to translate that into a working relationship would be two things. One, I think it would change the sort of domestic relationship in a way that I particularly wouldn't relish. But also, it would create an atmosphere around the two of us that would be difficult for others to engage with. I can't imagine being a clergy person in Jo's diocese, for example. I just don't think that's fair on the other clergy in the diocese. But I appreciate that couples who are both in ministry have to navigate these issues in their own way. We've been approached several times by people for advice and mentorship and guidance, and we've always said no. We have no wisdom on this. You've got to make your own arrangements. There is no magic formula.

SH: As far as we're concerned in those regards, Paula has always refused to be a German professor's wife. She doesn't go when I go give a lecture. She doesn't come and say, "Oh isn't he wonderful." And I certainly prefer that. I think that kind of role that was there for women is just gone. And rightly so. There's a kind of freedom that comes from that that I deeply value. I think Jo's pretty much the same way.

SW: (*laughter*) When Jo had been working with Archbishop Justin in his office at Lambeth, and then she was appointed Bishop of Dorking, people said to her, but how will you be Bishop while you're still living in Trafalgar Square? They assumed that she would live in my house, even though she was a bishop. And you've just got to laugh about things like that and also realize it's actually possible not to overshare. You come up with phrases like, "I'm sure we'll work something out," which says all that needs to be said.

Conversation Six

Power / Feeling at Home / Running Away / Future Readers

MKL: We've talked about your shared project. Stanley, I wonder how you would explain or describe the nuance of Sam's project. What has Sam been trying to do? What does he do?

SH: To enact in an ecclesial context the full reality of the gospel by showing the difference it makes in the kind of lives we lead.

SW: Yep. I think that would cover what we both have been trying to do. I mean obviously mine on the ground, I'm not going to say applied or practical, which would be terrible things to say, but in terms of the sort of Venn diagram where our lives and ministries and projects overlap, that would describe it very succinctly, I think.

SH: I'm surprised I could come up with it that clearly. (*laughter*)

SW: I think there's something that probably we've both been criticized by others about which we ourselves might reflect on differently, and that's something about power. Because if you're not someone who treats race and class and gender as being, if you like, primary identity categories, determinative categories, and you want to place those within the context of baptism and church, as things you do regard as primary categories, then you're going to be accused of being ignorant or bypassing questions of power.

SH: Reactionary.

SW: All sorts of things. To put words in Stanley's mouth, or what I would say on Stanley's behalf is perhaps a better way to put it, is that Stanley began his career and has never ceased to be somebody who is fascinated by the virtues. And virtue and power are really the same word in different languages. And so, in terms of his anger with the contemporary American church, it's been an anger that it refused to recognize its power appropriately or refused to rest that power on its appropriate sources, perhaps Eucharist, prayer, formation, catechesis. Instead it has sought power in the wrong places and in the wrong ways. So he is talking about power, he's just not using it in the way that people use the word justice, or as a kind of cipher for a whole range of commitments which Stanley would regard as ways in which the church becomes captive to a discourse that isn't its own discourse and therefore loses the plot in many cases. And it's the losing of the plot that makes him so angry and the neglect of the truly vital sources of power. While I agree with all of that, that's Stanley's bag, not mine.

My bag on that is pastorally rooted. From the very beginnings of pastoral ministry, the one theme that goes through all my different appointments is powerlessness—how all the different social contexts have brought me face to face with how both the people obviously on the underclass estate felt powerless, but then I moved to Cambridge, where even the famous professors themselves in some cases were only aware of how powerless they were. They were either locked in the university and couldn't affect public policy or they could transform the engineering of Tanzania but seemed to have no effect on the poverty levels in the country or whatever. And again, coming to Duke, the Nobel Prize winners at Duke all knew it had been a bad year and that actually if it'd been a good year they wouldn't have gotten it.

And so, I think my take on that has been always to resist accounts of power that are too wooden, hence the improvisation stuff, so much of which is about how the servant can exercise a power that the master can never attain. And I've found that sort of fascinating. How the word "sorry" can become such a power-fully manipulative word, whereas you think it was a low status word and therefore a person who says sorry is obviously in the wrong and therefore lacks power and so on. So I'm very inter-ested in power. But I'm almost never prepared to say the things about power that you're kind of expected to say.

When people do make the journey that Stanley's described of seeing the difference Christ makes, of receiving the gifts of the Spirit (or however you phrase it) and how empowered they can become by joining the kind of team of the church, and they sense where their own identity becomes secondary to a project that they're part of together and then how their own sense of powerlessness can be transfigured, transcended, by a sense of how God is working in the world of which they are perhaps spectators, perhaps interested onlookers, perhaps minor parts in a much bigger play, and how that changes their notion of their own powerlessness—those are the kinds of things I think run constant throughout the twenty-eight years or so of ordained ministry that I've had.

A phrase I often quote is, "It's better to fail in a cause that will finally succeed than succeed in a cause that will finally fail." That sentence pretty well encapsulates what I mean about the transi-tion in feeling you're part of a cause that will finally succeed as being part of the church. It's being with the grain of the universe, to use a phrase Stanley uses and is the title of one of his books.

SH: It's interesting. I've never thought of myself as powerless. I have thought of myself, almost from the beginning, as not belong-ing in the academy because of class issues. And I've always said, every class I've ever been in there's always been someone smarter, but no one works harder than I do. Part of my work has been the attempt to have power by being academically damn good. And

I'm not going to apologize for that. I think it's part of the world in which you live. Of course, to be academically good means that you made a mistake when you became a Christian ethicist because what does it mean to be a good scholar as a Christian ethicist? At least I've had to know what my enemy knows in a way that they don't have to know what I know, and that's been power.

MKL: You talk about not belonging in the academy because of class issues, and the ways your involvement with the academy distanced you from your parents. Where do you feel most at home? What places know you well? Where do you most fully belong?

SH: I don't want to idealize. I mean, I feel at home cutting my yard. I feel at home with Faith and Hope, the cats. I like living with Paula. I feel at home there. But where I feel most determinatively at home is Sunday morning at Holy Family. I mean that's really home in a way that I don't know if I could live without it. To have the liturgy form you and participate in that way is home for me. I never think of myself as a very impressive Christian, and I'm never quite sure I am. But on Sunday morning at ten o'clock, I am. I'm at home.

SW: I could give a lot of different answers to this question. Preaching at Duke Chapel (obviously not on day one) brought together the ecclesial and theological and academic, and there was a sense of making that my own. For that period of time, I felt at home in that role. Even though it's a much more contested space, I feel very much at home doing these broadcasts on radio, even though it's six million people and slightly nerve-wracking and you meet some weird and wonderful people in the green room and you get hostile emails afterwards almost always regardless of what you said.

I listened to that when I was twelve years old. My mother gave me a radio for my tenth or eleventh birthday, and I had the radio by my bed, and I would listen at twelve minutes to eight to

Thought for the Day just as I was going off to school. So I listened to that all my thinking life. And I'll be honest, times towards the end of my teenage years I thought, I could do that. And now to be asked to do that—and it doesn't get old because it's a fresh thing every time—rising to the challenge of doing that in a language that isn't preachy and doesn't have the conventions of church around it, and is very respectful towards the secular perspective—looking back forty-plus years to myself getting my first radio and first listening to it, I'm glad I'm now doing that. So there's a similar kind of feeling to it, and there's a home-ness to it.

I've never made any secret that there are parts of being vicar at St. Martin's that are really quite challenging, but St. Martin's has moments, particularly at worship—not just in worship by any means, but particularly in worship—that express glimpses of the kingdom more than anywhere else I think I've ever been. So, for example, on Palm Sunday when my colleague Richard has produced a play that involves maybe forty actors of the Passion, in which Jesus is played by an Afghan refugee and the Sanhedrin are played by more Anglo members of the congregation, and the disciples are played by people in wheelchairs and people who are asylum seekers, I am proud of those moments. This is more than just talking about inclusion, or kingdom, or work of the Spirit, or whatever language comes most easily. This is a beautiful thing. This would make Jesus smile.

SH: I just thought a few minutes ago that my answer has got to be self-deceptive, because where am I most at home? In my office! (*laughter*) And in the university. Certainly, I've been at home there. And I'm no good at retirement because the university has just been such a part of my life.

SW: Yeah, I mean if I was to be cruel to Stanley, I would say that he is the Methodist who is still struggling for a theology of grace. You noticed he said ten minutes ago that he works harder than the others.

SH: Right.

SW: And retirement is a moment of grace. There is no striving. And Stanley does not know who he is without that striving. Paradoxically, for Methodists grace can be overused but I don't think on a personal level Stanley's ever gotten it. And yet, there's a kind of addiction about it because it's always just out of reach. I don't think you've ever thought in crude terms about the next appointment, or the next award, or the next book will ever get you there.

SH: No.

SW: Because it's not externally validated. It's always an internal issue for Stanley in terms of being credible in his own eyes more than anything else.

SH: I do think about the future. I'm not sure how my work, if it will be read, how it will be read in the future because I am a determined dialogical thinker. I think in relationship to other thinkers and so my work is always engaging work that isn't mine and becomes mine through the engagement. For example, if you don't know who John Rawls is and what he stands for and the arguments he has made, I think it's not clear you will understand some of the arguments that I've made. So I don't know how that will work in the future because you will need to know too much to know how to read me. I think Sam's work is more likely to be read in the future because it's more direct and not as dependent on other voices. Do you think that's right, Sam?

SW: Whether it's read or not, I have no idea. But I think the difference is definitely spot-on. It's just a different way of doing things. You've just got to learn from failure and not to try to be a bad version of somebody else. I couldn't do what Stanley does. And for everybody it's a journey to say that's okay.

SH: I love *Improvisation* and how Sam uses improvisation categories. Blocking is such a powerful image and the examples he gives of blocking are so compelling. I think that that's going to be intelligible to readers fifty years in the future. I'm not sure what I try to do will be intelligible to readers fifty years in the future.

MKL: Do you perceive any part of your work as an attempt to run away? Are there pieces from your past that your work is trying to help you get away from?

SW: I think for Stanley that whole Methodist "giving your life to Jesus every Sunday night" thing is something he's running away from. And I think that's very significant. I had a difficult experience when I was nineteen, which is in the public domain and I've written a tiny piece about it which appeared in *Face to Face,* and the person at the center of the story died recently so it maybe feels a bit easier to talk about it. But I was part of a community where it's now come to light that there was abuse taking place. And obviously I have had to reflect on whether I experienced anything I've since suppressed, and I've not finished the journey on that. I've had to talk to the police at a great length of time, and the person who's recently died spent a period of time in prison but he was probably the first mentor that I had of significance. He presented me with a Christianity significantly different from what I'd grown up with but yet was very attractive and compelling. It was probably seven or eight years before the abuses came to light, in which time I was much less crucially affected by that experience. What I'm saying in all of that is if I'm running away from something, I think it's related to that very formative time.

Stanley always has a red light when it comes to the word "pious" or that side of Christian life, which I think brought me in touch with the paradoxical and painful juxtaposition of a real striving for holiness with a perversion, and the painful difficulty in telling them apart at times. That idea that we're all on the spectrum from the mass murderer over here to the very pious and devoted person with a life of purity here—I can't sustain that. I'm not surprised when I find even the most exalted people have profound flaws.

I'm still in touch with two people in particular, very close friends, but also others influenced by him who've all reacted in a host of different ways—some who have dismissed him as being rotten to the core, and others who are still upholding that it was all misconstrued. And I think I'm somewhere in the middle. I still think things that I learned from him are valid, in a sort of Augustinian non-Donatist way. The good that he did still has a validity, and I am still inspired by some parts of that. But clearly he had a malign effect on some people, and to the extent that wasn't me, I don't know why it wasn't me. He certainly had plenty of access, and I was certainly at a vulnerable point in my life, six months or so after my mother had died.

Running away from would be too strong, but since all of that, I've been trying to found a committed and passionate Christian commitment that isn't over-dependent on one charismatic individual or isn't blown apart by finding that people are human beings, and sometimes not very good human beings. So when Stanley talks about a community of character, that sense of community for me isn't an idealized thing, where there is an astonishing leader and everybody is devoted. It's more a place where we've all got strengths and faults and in an ideal way we can help others through.

I think possibly also, the other thing would be that little church that was so important to me as a child. I have a kind of complex relationship with churches of that kind, in the sense that I have never wanted to be the vicar of a church like that. It is probably very representative of the Church of England, but I've tended to do either churches that have a lot of poverty issues around them or now St. Martin's, which has all sorts of center of London dynamics. But there is something about going back to that sort of church of my childhood that frightens me because I guess it infantilizes me. That's probably the truth of it, as I can't work out how to be an adult in that environment.

SH: I think what I fear is being uninteresting. I want to be interesting because I don't want to bore myself. I hate boredom. Our lives are fundamentally conventional, or I think they're conventional, but I don't want to be trapped by that conventionality. I don't know any other way to live than the way we live, but I don't want to turn it into a project that would make the thinking through of Christianity impossible. That's what I fear, namely being bourgeois. (*laughter*) I don't want that.

Sam, changing the subject a bit, one of the things that I think is interesting about how we do theology and in particular, given the differences that are certainly there, is that neither of us are that interested in the technical issues within the theological framework. Neither of us spends that much time trying to give more adequate accounts of, for example, how Jesus [is] very God, very man in terms of two natures. We just want to assume that that's all okay, and we need to go on somehow. Do you think that's an appropriate characterization?

SW: Yes, I think it is. The whole Jesus seminar sort of stuff, I think you would just describe it as boring, right? It's just not something I've given a lot of attention to.

SH: If you take Rowan's recent book, *Christ the Heart of Creation*, where he starts with Aquinas's account of two nature Christology and how it works within his overall framework of creation—I need books like that, but I don't want to write them.

SW: I agree. I'm very glad that someone of Rowan's caliber is writing a book of that depth on that kind of a subject, and I do look at those books for my own purposes, in a sense that I don't regard those matters as closed. I think there's every reason why a theologian of his caliber should be writing a book like that. I don't have a longing to do that myself, but I'm glad to read it.

SH: Do you think there's a danger in the fact that we don't do it? I think of Lewis Ayers's book on the trinity, which again is a terrific scholarly book, theologically very astute, but it's not the kind of book I would want to write. I couldn't do it because I don't have the scholarly skills.

SW: Well, you do in a different way to Lewis. I'm not saying you couldn't do it. I would be glad for you to. I really enjoyed you doing *Matthew*, and I really enjoyed you doing *With the Grain of the Universe*, which was actually in many ways a philosophical theology.

SH: It was. That's true.

SW: But you didn't present it as that. You presented it as a few more things wrong with Niebuhr, and I think it was a lot more than that.

SH: I don't think what I did with *With the Grain of the Universe* has yet been received. I think that's a much better book than its reception [implied].

SW: Well, it's a book, whereas most of what you've done has been collections of essays, and this is a book with a big thesis—a very big thesis. But I think it would be easy to miss that if you just flipped through it.

SH: I'm not sure I could have done it any other way, but people now commenting on what I'm doing don't go back and read *Vision and Virtue* and see the importance of Wittgenstein and the importance of description as part of the philosophical formation. You need to go back and do *Vision and Virtue*, *Truthfulness and Tragedy*, and *Character and the Christian Life* to see how it becomes an ongoing project. Doing a book like Rowan's book wouldn't necessarily help if you didn't go back and do that earlier work. I've resisted ever trying to write a book on pulling it all together because I want people to have to go through the work that I've had to go through to get where you get.

SW: Yeah, and that's why the fact that people have caricatures of you is almost an inevitable result because they haven't done that much work.

SH: It's my fault. (*laughter*)

SW: I said it was an almost inevitable consequence. I didn't say fault.

SH: But it also has to do with having a sense of what will be the effect in the future. I'm appreciative of all the people that have written on me. I think Sam's book was very important for people getting a sense of the stages. But there are now beginning to be books, like Dean's book and Hunsicker's book on Barth and myself. I think I am beginning to be read with more understanding by this generation because the presuppositions about where Christianity is and the world in which we now find ourselves that I was presuming and drawing on now are clearly seen.

SW: Well, to put it in simple terms, there's a question: are you coming from where I'm coming from, or are you going where I'm going? And it is now difficult for people of this sort of generation to understand where you're coming from, to understand what you were angry with in the mid-70s. Situation ethics is no longer in the vocabulary. That whole set of disputes that was so formative to you and to which you were such an alternative voice—the whole virtue thing being such a contrast to the obsessions of the 60s—I think it's going to be very hard for people to understand where you're coming from. But that doesn't mean that it won't be very helpful for people to go where you're going.

SH: Right.

SW: So your constructive work around community and tradition and character and virtue, and then the concrete examples of how that plays out in medical ethics, disability, and in a hundred other ways, people will probably continue to draw on that. In a sense it's nice that someone's doing some work on you and Barth, if they feel you can draw a straight line from Barth to you, which in theory you should be able to do because Barth died in 1968 and you started writing around 1969. But there isn't really a straight line from you to Barth.

SH: Oh yes. Right.

SW: It goes through H. Richard Niebuhr, and it goes through various other people, obviously Frei and Lindbeck. I did the best I could twenty plus years ago to trace some of those lines. I'd be very surprised if anyone else comes along and does that kind of work again. But great that they're seeing you as just go straight to Barth. That's fine. And there is a book on you and Wittgenstein.

SH: By Kallenberg.

SW: So at least that work's being done.

SH: There's a man, Alessandro Rovati, he is Italian, who came originally to study with me to read MacIntyre. And he wrote an MA thesis at the University of Milan on MacIntrye, and then he decided that he wanted to do his PhD on me. So he came back and I said, okay, I'll give you a reading course for a year, and we're going to begin with *Vision and Virtue* and read through it. And he wrote a terrific thesis from Milan, so people can read about it rather than read it.

Gerry McKenny, who is a moral theologian at Notre Dame, once told me Reinhold Niebuhr dominated the field in the first half of the twentieth century, H. Richard dominated the field ongoing, but you have dominated the field since their work. I don't know that that's true, but I hope it is. I hope it is. Because I think the agenda I tried to put forward, because remember, when I began there was no account of virtue or narrative at all.

SW: The difference is the Niebuhrs are patrician people, and you are an insurgent. And your successors are those who perceive the field to be hugely contested by race and gender, who in some ways are more insurgent than you, though in my experience are seldom as constructive as you, because your insurgent piece has hidden your constructive sense. I don't think dominated is the right word for Stanley.

SH: Right, right.

SW: So Stanley's inserted himself into almost every conversation, often in caricatured form. He certainly doesn't know everybody, but almost everyone knows him.

Conversation Seven

Preaching / Sermon Prep / Nonviolent Arguments /
Sermons We Never Hear

MKL: Both of you have preached a lot of sermons. Do you remember the very first sermon you ever preached?

SH: Yes. I do. I remember it very well. I had gone and dedicated my life to Jesus at the altar, and I was about fifteen or sixteen. And it had become a tradition at Pleasant Mound Methodist Church that those that had dedicated their life to Jesus and usually assumed were going in the ministry, should preach a sermon on Sunday night. So my time came up. I was scared shitless. I had no idea what you should do. I went to the church library and I found a book of sermons by somebody named Harry Fosdick. It was called, *A Faith for Tough Times*. And so I copied out one of his sermons and I preached it. So my first sermon was by a good Protestant liberal.

SW: And included no doubt compelling phrases such as, "and all of us in New York would no doubt agree . . ."

SH: (*laughter*) Right. Right. I think I edited those out. I do remember I added something about alcohol and that you shouldn't drink.

SW: Commendable. I'll tell about my first sermon. It was in Liverpool. It was the year after university, before I went to seminary, and I was preaching on Remembrance Sunday, November 1987 to a group of about twelve or fifteen people, most of whom were of advanced years. There wasn't any organ or piano so I was choosing the hymns as I went along. And I can't remember the content of the sermon, but I do remember there was a woman who was nodding at all the bits that I thought were quite good and smiling at the bits that appealed to the heart, and she really seemed to be with the flow of it. So when it came to the offering I said, "This is Remembrance Sunday and for a lot of you this will be a significant Sunday in terms of loved ones who fought in the wars. And I wonder if any of you would like to choose a favorite hymn." And there was silence. And then I looked at the woman who'd been so carefully attending to my sermon and I said, "I wonder if you'd like to choose?" And then the woman next to her said, "Don't worry about her, love, she's deaf." So that was my first sermon.

MKL: Well, you've gone on to preach some more sermons.

SW: And there's been a lot of people who have been deaf who have nodded along at the right bits.

MKL: Tell me, how do you prepare differently for a sermon than a lecture? Or do you?

SH: I've never really thought about that. I spend more time writing a sermon than I spend writing an academic article. I usually write a sermon a month or two ahead, which is a great gift that I have that people in the ministry don't. I put down the scriptures and I xerox it, carry it around in my bag, and I read the scriptures all the time, trying to see how they might interrelate. Then I keep waiting for a way to contextualize the text in a way they narrate our lives and our world. I never try to get behind a text. For example, I recently heard a sermon commenting on Sarah's laughter, and speculation that the laughter must have been of sorrow, and all kinds of psychological theories, why as a woman suffering deprivation the laughter had to be bitter—I think all that is just bullshit. You never try to get behind the text.

You try to attend, in Richard Hays's phrase, to "how the words run." And I try to show how the words run in relationship to how the gospel is a narration of what it meant for Abraham to be the father of many nations. So I try to show the interrelationship of the text in a manner that helps illumine the world in which we find ourselves. I find sermons really offering the opportunity to be much more creative than most academic articles partly because it's not your opinion or your judgment. You're under the order of the text. So that's how I try to go about finding a sermon, and the word *finding* is important because it's not something that you necessarily create. You find it.

SW: So obviously this is something I've thought and written about a lot, and where in some way I've made myself unpopular with some people, not least when I spoke at a conference and I talked about the fact that in my process of preparing I look to six to ten commentaries or something, and a person in the audience said afterwards, "What about those of us who haven't got the time to do that?" And I said, "You've come to a session called 'Good to Great.'" It was a very Stanley sort of answer. Occasionally I give these sort of Stanley answers and they make me very unpopular. But I said, "Do you want to be a great preacher or don't you?"

To read six or ten commentaries is to have the humility to think that some other people in the history of the church have thought about this before you have. If you're not interested in two thousand years of exegesis, then good for you. But you're not going to be a great preacher. So a lot of people didn't like me saying that, and they didn't ask me back. I could have been a bit more polite, but occasionally I get these sort of Stanley-channeling moments and just tell it as it is.

Okay, so first principles. God has revelation to bring to this congregation today, and the definitive, although not exhaustive

way in which that revelation comes is from the scripture speaking today as urgently as it did when it was written in the first
century—just as the sacraments rely on the fact that they are
happening today and they're not just a memorial. I never use
an expression like "teaching sermon." To me that is the wrong
epithet. It's got to be revelation. What God has to reveal to us
today is almost invariably about God and therefore theology
beats ethics every time. Almost every time. And therefore, people that assume that a sermon is an opportunity to harangue
people about what they should do have not only misunderstood
the responsibilities of the preacher, they misunderstood what a
sermon is. A sermon is tearing the heavens open that we should
be able to better see God.

So then there are broadly three kinds of sermons. As I look at
the three scriptural texts set aside for the Sunday (not usually the
psalm), I will be looking for one of three things. So number one is,
how does one of these passages reveal the whole purpose of God?
Number two, has one of these passages got a telling phrase that
is potentially transformative and carries far more than it appears
to carry? And number three, is there a way in which one of these
passages touches on and opens up to us a contemporary question
in church or society that it's about time that a preacher in this
context addressed, particularly appropriate to a visiting preacher
who can run away afterwards? It's always easier than for the regular vicar or pastor.

I enjoy all of those and I try to have a variety between them.
But I think sometimes if you really can show how these nine
verses tell the whole of salvation history that it's very rewarding.
And I think Stanley likes those sermons because his tend not to
be like that.

SH: Sam and I agree that sermons must be arguments. That means
that you try to lay it out in a way that they see that what is being
said is confrontational in a way that you've got to give reasons

if you disagree. I think about sermons in terms of nonviolence because the sermon must be a proclamation of the revelation as Sam was suggesting, but if, for example, you say, "And you need to be because of the crucifixion nonviolent," they have no way of responding to say, "I don't get that."

So if you do that, it's a form of violence. They've got no response. So insofar as you can, raise an issue like why Christians have thought they've got a problem with war by creating a context in which that is implicated but is implicated in a way that's good news that they can think about. Hopefully the response to the sermon would be, "I've never thought about that." And so that's the kind of invitation to consider this in a way that isn't coercive because I think sermons can be didactic in a manner that leaves the hearer no place to be.

SW: I one-hundred percent agree that a sermon is an argument. And I become exasperated with the preaching that is always a kind of emoting or blogging on this is how the week seems to me, in no particular order. Preaching is taking the congregation's confusion about the scriptural passage and confusion about their lives and bringing order out of both, in harmony, or in fusion. It's not about taking their confidence about the scripture and all their lives and discombobulating it. I've heard so many sermons that say, "Ah, you think that 'rejoice' in Philippians 3 means the gospel is about being happy. But actually, it means be of good cheer. It means don't be discouraged. There's nothing happy about it." You know, how do you say amen at the end of that? This has got to be good news. The heart of it is addressing existential dimensions of people's ordinary lives and bringing clear points of Christian revelation into those. That's the heart of it.

MKL: What should we expect from a sermon? You both agree it should be an argument. Stanley, when you show up on Sunday morning, what are you expecting?

SH: That Christology is at the heart of it. That it be a response to the text assigned for that day, that it have something to say, and it avoids sentimentality. I say, as soon as a pastor says, "As I learned from my ten-year-old," you can forget it. It's gonna be bullshit. That's sentimentality.

I think humor is important. I don't have any problem with sermons being entertaining. I preached Maundy Thursday a few years ago at Holy Family and I started with the line, "Episcopalians don't come to church to be touched." (*laughter*) I caught them immediately because they were all sitting there thinking, *I don't want to have my feet washed* (because we wash everyone's feet). But they thought that was funny because I recognized who they were. And then I went on to talk about what it means to be touched by Jesus. So a sermon can be entertaining and funny and still substantive. What I don't understand is why do people go to Joel Osteen's church? I don't get it. I mean, what's alleged the sermon is about is simplistic and superficial.

SW: I think it's three reasons. Number one: they're part of a bigger event that transcends their mundane lives. Number two: they are given very practical guides of self-help to improve their lives. And number three: they are surrounded, as it appears, by successful people who have applied these principles and now who live life free of the anxiety and tawdriness that they know about their own.

SH: Boy, I can't believe that the children of those people will go to church. They'll see through it, surely.

I think how the sermon relates to the Eucharist is to be always thought about, in terms of suggesting that because of this, we do this. Calvin saw the sermon as more or less the introduction to the Eucharist. He used the language of sealing the sermon. I think that's a very interesting way to put the issue. The sermon is not just the preacher preaching. It is the reception of the Word by the congregation in a way that is analogous to receiving the body and blood.

SW: I think that one of Stanley's neglected books is the one he did with Willimon on preaching to strangers. In some ways, I regret we never did another one of those when I was at the chapel because that was one of the first of Stanley's books, and the first of Will's books, that I read. Stanley talks about the moral formation of a congregation, and how a sermon requires listeners, which I had never thought about before reading that book.

SH: The only people that have ever read that book are Clarke French, our rector at Holy Family, and you. You're the only two that have read it. (*laughter*) I do think that you preach to a congregation that should exist. And if it doesn't exist, you still preach to the congregation that should have existed to receive the Word. Therefore, it's a way of trusting the Word because the Holy Spirit is there to transform the Word in people.

SW: Yeah, and that Spirit means that when your spouse or friend says to you, "How did it go down?"—the answer is always, "I have no idea." Because you learn not to trust what people say to you at the door. And you know that what they said to you at the door only represents their own view, and it can't represent the view of the whole congregation. So you never know. And of course the other thing you learn when you know a congregation well is how easy it is to be preparing a sermon that speaks specifically to one person in the congregation who I can tell you for a fact will not be there on the Sunday when you preach that sermon. (*laughter*)

SH: Reinhold Niebuhr, in *Leaves from the Notebook of a Tamed Cynic*, said that preachers don't compromise the gospel in the sermons because of their fear that they will lose their position or their salary, but that it's very hard to preach the truth to people who are hurting and that you come to love. And I think that that is one of his very wise insights, about how it is that the minister oftentimes knows that this person is breaking apart because of the alcoholism of their spouse, and how do you preach the truth to someone in such pain? The answer is, with the truth of the gospel which is clothed in compassion.

What I fear oftentimes is a temptation of those of us who are quite critical of the contemporary church is we can be lured into contempt against the people that now make up the church. And contempt is a vice that invites you to feel superior to the people that you are serving. And I think the cynicism that oftentimes grips the lives of people in the ministry today that borders on contempt, is one of the things that we have to strongly resist.

MKL: So how do we resist that? How might clergy be formed in such a way to resist? What practices cultivate it?

SH: They have to be given a sense of what an important vocation they've been called to do. And it's going to take time. And that's what the gospel gives us: time. And they've got to love God and love the people God has put before them.

SW: Most of my articles that I regularly write in *The Christian Century* are actually trying to address that question. Ministry consistently confronts you with your impetuous and inappropriate judgments about people, and makes you see them much more textured than you ever considered. It puts you to shame.

So I think the question that we haven't talked about preaching which I feel is in the air is everything that talks about learning styles and multimedia presentations, and everything that says basically preaching is something on a spectrum from an abuse of power through to impossible for people to engage with because it's not done on a mobile device.

I'm sure those kinds of discourses are alive in seminaries all over the place, to which my response is, think about when you have profoundly changed your mind or profoundly discovered something. And it more or less comes down to two ways in which we change our minds or have a sense of discovery. One is where somebody has walked with us in sort of an Emmaus Road kind of way and listened to us and enabled us to see things from our own experience—a sort of therapy type situation. And in the tea leaves of our experience, we have found wisdom that we didn't realize. The other would be, whether it's the TV program or the teacher in class at school, where somebody from outside has given us a gift about which we had no previous conception. We had no idea that the chemical reactions on a planet in another solar system were so fascinating, shall we say. I would defend preaching that's well done is a version of the second, that has the power of conversation, which in the end, as we started off by saying, is the fundamental form of human interaction.

But that doesn't mean that it can't be helpfully sprinkled and modified by such learnings of the first. If the preacher understands your existential yearnings and can say something like, "There are many anxieties in our life but they really come down to two," and [if you] then render those in language that people would themselves recognize, then I think you've done about as good a job as you can do.

So I didn't think I would be defensive and say, usually pronounced in a Scottish accent, "Preaching the Word still stands the test of time." I don't think we can use sort of big talk to defend something if it's culturally inaccessible to people. But there is nothing more compelling than a single spoken voice. It's like a single sung voice. An *a cappella* individual singer holding a microphone singing a song is as good as it gets . . . if it's a wonderful song and they've got a wonderful voice. So likewise, I would say, trust the process, provided you've got something fabulous to say. And the gospel, when you tell it, has got to be good and it's got to be news.

SH: I think one of the problems with preachers that are fundamentally burned out is they fear their congregations. They're not sure that they're capable of understanding what they have to say, and they don't want to make anyone feel bad. So they preach nostrums about how to get through life—simplicity that everyone knows is just useless. You know, "Be kind." Do you need a preacher to tell you to be kind? I mean, that's not even necessarily good advice. (*laughter*)

SW: That's not advice Stanley's ever taken terribly seriously.

SH: So, I think how to convince people to trust God, and then you trust God will help you trust how the Word is to be formed in the congregation, is a fundamental formation that people need to receive as a part of being part of the ministry of the church. Hopefully we can do it through seminary though I don't think we do it very well. I don't approve of seminarians preaching in the chapel. I don't think that's a good idea.

SW: Get Stanley on the subject of student preacher Sunday.

SH: I think it's putting the student on the spot that says usually, let me show you how much I've learned. That's not good for them or good for us in terms of how the sermon turns out.

MKL: Does your preaching differ in any way because one of you is ordained and one of you is not?

SW: Mine's better.

MKL: (*laughter*) Yes. that's exactly what I was looking for: whose is better?

SH: Well I'm not ordained.

MKL: Right. So does that make a difference in terms of the sermons you and Sam preach?

SH: I hope I try to assume the same responsibilities that the ordained assume, which is, I'm not preaching my opinion. I'm preaching the gospel of the church through the ages. I do not any longer spend much time looking at contemporary commentaries. I find they say the same damn thing that I learned in Introduction to the New Testament when I was a seminarian.

SW: You're reading the wrong ones.

SH: I do read ancient commentaries, which usually have an oddity that gives you imaginative possibilities. But to go through one more time whether Mark had or did not have Q . . .

SW: I don't read the ones that talk about things like that. I do think that clergy need regular reminder that laypeople take the gospel as seriously as they do. It continually comes as a surprise to clergy. And so to have someone like Stanley, or Ellen Davis, who are probably the two lay preachers I have heard and most enjoyed, is a really healthy reminder to take your congregation seriously for all the talents both ministerial and missional that they've been given, and also as a refresher for yourself. Often they exhibit qualities that you've either forgotten or never had.

Unfortunately, though, it can then generate an idea that it's good for us all to have a go. I have known a church where when you ask people what they liked about the preaching they would say, "We really appreciate the variety of voices." They couldn't actually tell me any of them had been any good. And so I'm suspicious of variety because it's not a virtue in its own right. It can be a way of hiding.

SH: If I might blow my own horn: I think I did at St. Thomas Church Fifth Avenue the seven last words of Jesus. It's called *Cross-Shattered Christ*. It's a series of sermons that I'm quite happy with and it's where you can see theology being done as part of the sermonic display. And I learned much from engaging those words. I was particularly happy with "It's Finished," in the sense that it's not Jesus saying, well I'm dying, I'm dead. But the cross is the great victory, the kingdom is here. It is finished. I've done what I've set out to do. I would have not been able to write the commentary on Matthew if I hadn't done that preaching.

One of the things you discover is the inexhaustibility of scripture, and scripture is inexhaustible because God's inexhaustible and so you can preach over the same text year after year in a way that you never burn it out. There's always something more.

SW: Yeah, I'm not quite as confident as Stanley is. Theologically, obviously, I agree. I preach quite a lot in the Old Testament these days, and part of that is theological conviction that the Old Testament is the gospel. And part of it is the reality that I've probably preached on the gospel a good couple of times in public settings, and I've said most of what I have to say. (*laughter*)

SH: I know. I appreciate that.

SW: So I know in theory it's inexhaustible, but in practice, to retain that sense of freshness, dynamism. I think that's another thing that's an Anglican obsession that I don't share: this idea that you somehow miraculously need to show how you've woven together all three passages. I just don't share that. The result I think is either something that is really obscure that is lost on the congregation, or it's impoverishing what each individual text has got to give by trying to sort of cream off the bits that relate to each other.

SH: I've tried. I really have tried.

SW: I know you've been sort of lulled into that. I really resist that. I mean obviously there are occasions, particularly at festivals, and to be fair the former Church of England lectionary encouraged that and I think a whole generation of clergy therefore came to regard that as normal, but I've really resisted that. I want to hear what this passage has to say, even if it jars against what we think it's supposed to say, and I don't know how you do that if you're trying to constantly harmonize the dissonant voices.

SH: Surely one of the problems of contemporary preaching is that it is so seldom on the Old Testament.

SW: Yes. The Old Testament wasn't even read when I came to St. Martin's.

SH: I always think of Peter Maurin's phrase, "The church is sitting on the dynamite of the gospel." And in the sermon what an opportunity you've got every Sunday and oftentimes it turns out to be a firecracker rather than the dynamite.

MKL: There's not enough preaching from the Old Testament. What other sermons do we rarely hear preached today, but you think we ought to?

SH: You never hear a sermon on war. You never hear a sermon on marriage. You never hear a sermon on the catechism of children. You never hear a sermon on death. I think funerals are one of the most important times for preaching, in which a life is narrated through the gospel, which oftentimes is not possible other than as pathos. You never hear a sermon on atheism. We rarely hear a sermon on the failure of love. That's a good enough list.

SW: I'm glad to say I've covered most of those in published territory, but I think that's a great list. I certainly remember when I preached two sermons on heaven and hell at the chapel, and I got more responses to those for the very reason Stanley said. Money, sex, and power are the most obvious ones and if these really are the dynamics of people's imaginations, and if you're not talking about them, you've got to ask yourself why not. How to pray. Unanswered prayer. Healing. There's a lot of confusion about that. If we really have no expectation that people are going to stand up out of wheelchairs and walk out of the church, why do we advertise our annual healing service that creates that expectation? There has to be some theological engagement with the complexity of that in a positive way. Artificial intelligence. I've yet to hear a sermon on that.

I think the problem of division in the church as a theological problem and the delay in the coming of Christ—already/not yet isn't a sufficient answer to that. There seem to be clear expectations in the New Testament that this was all going to be wrapped up with a few people's lifetimes, and it hasn't yet happened.

I think people really respect a preacher that mentions the bit that every preacher they've ever heard preach on that passage has dodged because there's no nice moral to be derived from it. Why does everyone get slaughtered at the end of Esther? What kind of kingdom does this portray? I really do think you earn people's respect by being fearless and saying there is God's Word to be heard from every verse. The ghastly smiting of the Babylonian children's heads in Psalm 137.

MKL: We probably don't want to end a chapter with those words.

SW: (*laughter*) No. This probably wouldn't be a good place to end.

Conversation Eight

Murder Mysteries / Nationalism / Baseball / Competition /
Forgiveness / Life-Saving Friendships

MKL: Who are the two of you reading right now about whom you have not yet written?

SH: Is there anyone I have not written about or used? (*laughter*) I've been reading for a lecture I'm to give about the issue of friendship with the intellectually disabled. So I've been going back and reading Reinders and Swinton—people who have written very intelligently on the subject. I always read MacIntyre. His *Ethics in the Conflicts of Modernity* is just brilliant. It's a very important book to me. I've been reading David Bentley Hart's translation of the New Testament, which is a real kick in the gut. It's really terrific. And I've been reading murder mysteries.

MKL: Murder mysteries? Tell us about murder mysteries.

SW: I'm amazed Stanley's not exhausted that genre. He's read so many.

SH: You cannot exhaust that genre.

SW: He's read so many. So, Robert Heaney has written a book of post-colonial theology. So that's what I'm working on at the moment. Unlike Stanley, I'm not reading ten great books at a time, apart from novels which I always read—I get a lot of enjoyment from novels.

MKL: I'm curious about the novels as well. Stanley, I've heard stories about your love of Trollope's work and your desire to reread all of his books. Did you in fact do that? Or are there novelists you find just as fascinating that you would aspire to reread?

SH: Trollope himself said he was not particularly good at plots, but I think he was a great novelist because he had extraordinary judgment about people and had a way of writing kindly even about people he disliked. So I am very attached to Trollope. As I say, I've been reading primarily murder mysteries. People have never attended to an essay that I wrote—

SW: "McInerny Did It"?

SH: Yes, where I ask whether pacifists should read murder mysteries because you necessarily are sympathetic with the detective and you want murderers to be caught. I think pacifists ought to want murderers to be caught. It doesn't mean you kill them, but it means you enact justice. So how you give an account of that is very challenging. I liked what I did in that essay, though few people have taken it up.

MKL: Have you ever considered writing a novel?

SH: No. Many people late in life think, the hell with it, I'm tired of doing this kind of stuff I've been writing all my life, I'm going to write a novel. But it takes a lot of training and skills to write a novel, and I haven't been undergoing that so I'm certainly not going to try. I did think that *Hannah's Child* is novelistic and the style that I used is novelistic, but it's not a novel.

MKL: Stanley, you said some wish you would have written more about race, and although you haven't done so, you still continue to read people who are. Who would you recommend? Who does the church need to be listening to?

SH: My colleague here in Religious Studies, Joe Winters, has just written a very fine book on race. It's an account of the American situation that talks about the blues in relationship to coming to terms with racism and the hardness of any "solution." So it takes the tone of lament that I think is a very fine book. Coetzee has these accounts that there is no solution to racism in America. And there are then the developments of what is known as racial nihilism by African Americans who see no way out, which I think you need to take seriously, but hopefully that's not the last word. And then one of my former students and friends is Jonathan Tran, and he's writing a book on yellow racism, as a way to try to show that it's a mistake to cover what happened to Asian folks through the lens of racism against African Americans.

MKL: How about you, Sam?

SW: Was it not you who recommended Ta-Nehisi Coates to me?

MKL: Yes. I told you about *Between the World and Me.*

SW: So I read that, and that would count in the nihilism territory that I think Stanley is describing. It's a hard thing to say, but the particular dynamic of the United States post-slavery, of white on black racism, is in many respects a United States phenomenon. So being based in London the last seven years, it hasn't been an issue that's occupied my attention as much as it did when I was here. It doesn't mean it's not a very serious issue. It's just not been an issue that has taken my full attention in a way that the legacy of British imperialism and its continuing global and local effects seems to be an area I need to be thinking more about. Obviously when I'm sitting in North Carolina, it doesn't feel quite like that. But the dynamics of race in Britain are just different.

MKL: I'm not sure I know the best way to ask this question but as a white Christian in the United States today, in the midst of white nationalism and white supremacy, what are the questions I *should* be asking? What does discipleship look like?

SH: I think that you work very hard at DePauw and Greencastle to make life there better. And that means open to diverse groups of people that have been excluded. That's part of the thing you do. You don't try to solve the problem of something called America. You just try to make life in Greencastle better. I don't think that is a formula of defeatism, but rather it is a formula, or a way of responding, that helps avoid the presumption that there's nothing we can do. There is something you can do. I think what I've just been saying is the kind of background of the IAF (Industrial Areas Foundation) way of going about caring for the world, and I think that's a very good model. Luke Bretherton's new book, by the way, *Christ and the Common Life*, is a very important book that tries to give alternatives. It may still be at a rather abstract level, but it's well worth engaging.

SW: Well, I again think story is a crucial part of this. There's something in common between the populist story, as it's often described now, that unites some aspects of the Brexit movement in Britain and the Trump phenomenon, particularly the sense of anger of dispossession that there was something that rightfully belonged to people which has by unseen forces been taken away, and the presence of people not like us infesting our lives is one of the most damaging symptoms of the fact that we are now dispossessed. That story coming out of the sort of post-industrial parts of America and Britain seems to be similar. It's obviously got its own features and the people not like us dimension has got its own dynamics to the extent that that's either true or who those people are. It's very hard to engage that story and build on its most attractive elements because there aren't many.

SH: I was standing years ago at Bayswater and the street that runs by Kensington Gardens. Maybe it's Oxford? I was standing there on the corner and a little lady came up. She was about five feet, two inches, and she had her string bag and she heard my accent and she turned to look at me and she said, "This was a fine area of London before these blacks moved in." And I thought, *A little lady expressing that kind of racism?* And it suddenly occurred to me the Brits weren't free of racism.

SW: Oh no. And when you're changing a narrative you've got to talk about where it's coming from and where it's going. It's plenty easy to problematize where it was coming from, just as it is for church nostalgia. We look back to the 50s which are supposed to be the promised land, but it was clearly profoundly racist and sexist in ways that almost everybody today would find problematic. And where's it going? Where is this very unattractive narrative going to that starts from a place of such inflexibility towards difference? Whereas difference can only be seen to me as a form of dynamism and energy and spark, but there's no doubt that postindustrial change has left significant parts of the country behind and it's not entirely clear whose responsibility that is. But it shouldn't be entirely surprising that that has not gone unnoticed by local populations.

The question is about identity more than economics. I think the mistake that was made by certainly British politicians was the assumption that if people were reasonably well-off they would be reasonably happy. But there are more fundamental things, and clearly a number of people in recent elections and particularly in the Brexit referendum voted against their own economic interests because there was something more important to them, not always because they were foolish and stupid and ignorant to their economic interest, but they realize there is something more fundamental. And I actually think that's a good thing. I just disagree about what those fundamental things are. But having the conversation on identity feels to be something the church should be very comfortable about because identity is a big part of what we're in the business of.

But there's almost a meta-theological dimension to this in the sense that Christians believe in the Trinity. They believe that ultimate truth is in some significant degree plural and is about the harmony of unity and plurality that the Trinity represents. So homogeneity is neither a glorious thing to look back to nor a glorious thing to look forward to.

SH: What's the congregation at St. Martin's like in terms of having people that are not white?

SW: In terms of British congregations, outstanding I'd say. But the question would be, is that sufficiently represented in the leadership?

SH: This is one of the places that classical Christian convictions that could appear quite conservative turn out to be very radical. Once you have a catholic understanding of the church then borders make no sense. So what the immigration issue means for how Christians understand their place in the world is very significant. Because even though we're Americans, we're Christians, which means as Christian Americans we have to say border crossing is what we do. It's called catholic. And therefore we have to help those who fear immigration.

MLK: How might we offer such help? What does it look like in today's context to model a better story specifically for those who fear immigration?

SH: How to help those who fear immigration is to remind them they are Christians. Christians are never at home in the world. They are always on the move. That movement has always been the church's most effective evangelism.

SW: You've highlighted this by saying so unambiguously things like, "The subject of Christian ethics in America in the twentieth century has always been America," thus clearly problematizing national identity as being in any way in the Premier League of Christian concerns. To say Stanley's writing against a whirlwind is an understatement. I've never forgotten, traveling with an intern down to let's just say an eastern part of North Carolina in my first semester at Duke and then preaching a sermon and engaging with the community and then on the way back we talked inevitably about how there are American flags in the sanctuary and he said to me, "Dean Wells, you may be under the impression that nationalism is the way we express our Christianity. The truth is that Christianity is the way we express our nationalism."

MKL: Speaking of national stories, Stanley, this is your chance to say something about baseball.

SH: I've done baseball with Sam, and he will never get it. He thinks it's a slow game where nothing is happening. But cricket, there's a lot happening even though it's a slow game. The kind of game I'd like to teach him is Texas 42 dominoes. It's a kind of bridge domino. Have you ever played it?

MKL: I haven't.

SH: You pick four players. Take seven. You partner and call a trump, and you try to take all the tricks that are fives because those are the point dominoes. It's a Texas game because there were domino players around Mount Pleasant in the town square because Texans could play dominoes, but they couldn't play cards because Southern Baptists said cards are sinful. So how you learn to play dominoes was everything having to do with your religious convictions. And so that's what I'd like to teach Sam. Because he's very competitive.

SW: So my friends tell me. I never agree to that.

MKL: Is there a place for competition in Christian community?

SH: Absolutely. I played church softball into my sixties and we always wanted to win, though we lost well. St. Thomas More always had more good players than we had. The AME church also took it much more seriously than we did. So it's fun, as long as you don't take winning and losing as some kind of ultimate judgments. I think also that there's a kind of competitive process as part of being academics that isn't all bad. That you want to be as good as so-and-so. I think competition can spur to interesting, imaginative developments. You're not competitive though, Sam, I know.

SW: I haven't heard him do this, but I can imagine Stanley saying something like, "The liberal project," to use a Stanley-type phrase, "has been one of establishing conditions of fairness such that we never need to negotiate the discomfort of finding ourselves either better or worse equipped to face life than our neighbor." That would be a sort of Stanley-type sentence.

SH: I could say that.

SW: I could imagine you saying something like that. Whereas playful competition is in a sense training for non-playful competition. That's why it's promoted in schools and things like that, and it brings accompanying virtues. Teamwork generates needing to use and unleash and discover the gifts of everyone on the team. And that's true of the factory, and it's true of the consultancy firm, and it's true in many contexts.

But the heart of it for me is what you do when the result is announced, whether it's Miss World turning to her failed neighbor, saying, "You're not as beautiful as me," or whatever context it might be, you've then got to find a way to live with yourself given that we all fail in the end, sooner or later. The people that find it hardest to retire from major sports are the people who've been the winners all along and then have to cope with the fact that they need to face the rest of life in which those kind of victories are no longer available to them.

SH: I think that these kinds of issues really come to the fore in your retirement. When you retire you can hear your power leaving because you no longer by your very existence demand attention. And you have to get used to what it means to be not in the forefront anymore, and I don't know if I've made that transition yet. But I know that it really exists. That you lose power. It means what you write, no one needs to read again. There's a loss in that and you can mourn it, but I suspect it's also a good thing for you to learn how to recognize you're no longer who you once were when you had the job.

MKL: You said there can be a healthy sense of competition, especially as an academic, which might prompt you to want to be as good as so-and-so. Who were the so-and-sos for you?

SH: To be as good as? I wanted to be as good as Paul Ramsey, Jim Gustafson. I want to be as responsive as Jeff Stout, in terms of how he's criticized me and creates thought. I've got friends that I don't know that I'm necessarily in competition with, but people who I would like to always feel like they need to read me, like Travis Kroeker at McMaster in Canada.

SW: You haven't mentioned Alasdair.

SH: Oh yes. I have a letter from Alasdair that I treasure. He wrote, saying he couldn't write for the Festschrift or be at the retirement event, but wanted to tell me how much my work has meant to him. And he said, "You have done a remarkable thing. You have made it difficult to be a Christian, and oftentimes theologians do not do that. And you have made it equally difficult to be a non-Christian, as you have presented an account of Christianity that has shown the difference that being a Christian makes, that puts the burden of proof on those who are not." I felt like I'd graduated from college to get that kind of a letter from Alasdair!

MKL: Sam, are there people in your life that you want to be as good as?

SW: (*pause*) I mean a very important person for me is a person I call Ben, but his proper name now is Father Chad. He's a monk at Ampleforth in Yorkshire. He was my best man. And I don't know if you know the book *Narziss and Goldmund* by Hermann Hesse, but it was a very significant book for me when I was eighteen or nineteen, in probably not terribly helpful ways. It is really a yin and yang book that portrays two characters whose lives go in different directions. Trouble about that book as it applies to Ben and me is that we've kind of gone in the wrong direction, according to the book. I was probably the more thoughtful one and I've gone into the world, and he was the more wild child and he's gone into the monastery.

SH: Do you still stay in contact with him?

SW: Oh yes. I still think of him as my closest friend, even though we can go months without corresponding. He was my first real sort of college close friend, I guess. And yet I know that my projections onto him have been projections; I mean, he doesn't feel he is the person that I always see him as. He would be a person that I both admired and enjoyed in the way that I've admired and enjoyed Stanley. If I didn't know Stanley, I would admire his work. He's a friend, and I still admire his work. That's sort of what I mean by admire and enjoy.

But I'm not making a long list of people whose good opinion I covet, if that's the question. It was nice when Walter Brueggemann said some extremely nice things about my work because he's a person that has got a very distinguished career and has provided extraordinary insights for an enormous number of people. So for him to use the superlatives that he used was unexpected and gratifying, I guess to use a rather strange phrase. I don't really believe it when people say nice things like that, but it's nice of them to say. And recently, as you know, a person formerly in authority over me said some nice things about some of my work, and because I respect him so much as a human being, his good opinion counted for a lot.

SH: Who?

SW: Graham James, formerly bishop of Norwich, wrote a nice review of *Walk Humbly*.

So it's nice to feel that such people think that I've got something to bring to the table.

SH: I think one of the things about that question is a little embarrassing to try to answer it, but what we do is so fragile and you're never sure you know what you're doing, so if you can get some affirmation from someone you really respect, you treasure it.

SW: So the question I ask myself is something like, who are the people who have formed my confidence about whether what I've done is good, such that I don't really need to ask them? Stanley would certainly be one of those. It's not a particularly long list, but there are a small number of friends who wouldn't have Stanley's qualifications, but who know when I'm being true to myself and true to my calling and when I'm not.

SH: There is the issue between what we think and how we live, and whether thought depends on the moral virtues, which is something we both on the whole think is right but is more complex than the formulas allow. Because we think thoughts that are more significant than our lives.

SW: I don't think there's a simple answer to those kinds of questions other than for me to reflect back on the journey I have made since I was nineteen, in the face of very close friends who feel very differently, that there was a person there whose ministry I still experience in significant ways as a blessing, nonetheless let a lot of people down.

And the three things to say about that I guess are, first of all the point we made earlier about Donatism and how Augustine talked about the effectiveness of the ministry not being inhibited by the weakness of the minister. That's the first thing to say. The second thing to say is forgiveness and reconciliation are at the center of the gospel, but that doesn't make them the easiest things. And the third thing is to say there are some circumstances in which the process of forgiveness and reconciliation has to be rightly delayed, withheld, postponed, in some cases, almost indefinitely because it can't be a mutual, reciprocal process.

SH: I've had a judgment about another person who I thought deeply wronged both someone I loved and also myself. And I've been called to question whether I shouldn't seek reconciliation through acknowledgment, and I refuse to do it. Because I said, I don't know this person has a soul sufficient to come to terms with the kind of challenge I would present. Maybe in heaven there can be reconciliation. But as far as I know now, I don't see what that would look like. Whether that is a position that should be taken, I don't know. But it's one I've taken, namely I just don't know that they have a soul sufficient to being able to be so confronted. These are serious matters. You can go ahead and be civil, but it doesn't mean that you accept their power over you in that way. Have you had that?

SW: Yeah. That last point about accepting their power over you—I'm thinking this is not an entirely good fit as a story, but it's a well-known story. It appears in different religions and in different forms, but the form in which I know it is that there are two monks walking in the forest and they come to a stream and they see a beautiful young nymph. And she asks if they will carry her across the stream, and one of them does and then puts her down and then they walk on through the forest. And then the one that didn't carry her says, "That was a terrible thing to do; we're taught as monks that we shouldn't put ourselves in a position of desire." And then the monk that did the carrying said, "I put her down on the side of the stream. It sounds like you're still carrying her."

To me a lot of the question about that kind of thing is, if somebody you feel has hurt you, and almost in every case you were not the totally innocent party if truth be told, but the person has for reasons of their own made your life unpleasant, possibly publicly, possibly material, forgiveness in a situation like that—particularly as Stanley puts, when you do feel you're dealing with a person who isn't rational or as Stanley put it in this occasion has a soul that can engage, then forgiveness isn't an all-or-nothing thing. But getting to the point where you're not still carrying the nymph, or as Nelson Mandela put it, "As I walked [out the door] toward the gate that would lead to my freedom, I knew if I didn't leave my bitterness and hatred behind, I'd still be in prison." The ability to let go of a thing like that, and no longer to be defined by the wrong done to you is not the whole of forgiveness but it's a very large chunk of it.

SH: Right.

SW: What you pray for is the grace to be able to put the nymph down on the side of the stream and not be still carrying her years or decades later because that is giving the person power over you, and to use a crude but common way of putting it, that means they've won.

SH: They won, exactly.

SW: When something is in the position where it can't be dealt with—maybe the person has died, or it's something that's beyond redemption, or their reactions are disproportionate and hurtful, the stage you're trying to get to is to be able to say, "I've actually put that down." Justice in the sense that everyone gets a sort of fairness cannot be achieved. The phrase that I've started to use about justice is "everybody wants justice for other people but they don't want justice for themselves." We want mercy for ourselves and justice for everybody else.

SH: People often say they can't sing the psalms that ask for justice against the enemy, but I always point out that that's because you won. Think of yourself as someone that's poor that hasn't gotten justice and wants God to do it. That makes a lot of difference. I think one of the things that's involved in this kind of discussion is the place of victimization.

That has now become an identity marker. I want to be victimized because I know who I am if I'm victimized, but that always lets your oppressor win because you cannot tell your story without telling the story of the oppressor. So one of the great contributions of Christianity is a way to try to tell your story in a way that doesn't let oppressors win. And that means there's got to be some form of resistance even when the resistance isn't noticed by your oppressor. These are extremely complex relations that must be modeled by people that you can imitate. If you think about, for example, the L'Arche movement, that in some ways was a way of learning from the core members who refuse to let the oppressor—their difference—determine who they are. That's a form of justice we can hardly imagine, and I think is at the heart of what it means to be a Christian.

SW: So I've sat next to Stanley in public settings where people have said ignorant things: "You know nothing about mental illness," when Stanley lived with a bipolar spouse for nearly twenty-five years. Or, "You have no respect for women," when it's hard to think of a professor who has modeled appropriate cherishing relationships with graduate students to the degree that Stanley has done. You just wonder, where are they getting this stuff from?

And I remember particularly the comment about mental illness, that Stanley didn't say, "You probably don't know much about my personal history," which he could have done and completely crushed the person, quite justifiably. But instead he responded at face value, saying, "You make an interesting point about the place of people with mental illness in the church, and the ways the church has been slow to recognize the gifts of people who sometimes present their gifts in challenging ways." I remember I just thought that was amazing.

And I have tried to learn from that. I very seldom, however combative somebody's written to me, bother to get into real dialogue. There's never something constructive. What's driving you is the competitive sense that I'm right and you're wrong.

MKL: This question appears in the second volume of the *In Conversation* series, and is a question Barbara Brown Taylor was once asked and is now fond of asking others: What is saving your life right now?

SH: Friends.

SW: I think I would have given the same answer.

SH: Friends that you know are there. And who know you well enough to know how to be there. It's very important.

SW: The answer I might have given at different times over the last thirty years would be story. It's not just the whole narrative conversation that's Stanley's work has promoted and I've followed in the slipstream. I think it's important for most of us to feel that the story your small work is a part of kind of horizontally, the other people that are working on this with you, including the two of you I would count in that (I feel we're doing the same thing together just in different contexts), but also the story going at ninety degrees to that, which is where am I coming from, where am I going, what's all this adding up to.

When you lose sight of the story, being able to sit down with friends who can re-narrate the story in ways that become compelling. Things in life don't always turn out as you hoped or expected, putting it in very simple terms. And you have to recalibrate that story. What I find I can't do is simply live without a story. I've got to feel this has meaning and purpose and direction. So friends who know who you really are, and what is circumstantial and transitory, and what is permanent. I don't know what I'd do without those people.

SH: I had a friend tell me recently that I let too many people in my life. And I suspect that's true.

But I don't know any other way to live. But one of the things that creates is a feeling that I'm oftentimes not as responsive to friends as I should be because I just am too busy with other friends. And so to say friends isn't an entirely innocent thing because more people claim me than I know, and they're potential friends and I don't quite know how to negotiate that.

Conversation Nine

Denominational Ambiguity / Ecclesial Commitments /
LGBTQ+ Identity / Premarital Counseling

SH: One of the aspects that we haven't talked about is our rather loose relation with denominational identities.

MKL: How do you make sense of that?

SH: Well, I take it as an indication of the character of the current ecclesial realities, namely denominationalism is over as far as I can see. No one is a Methodist because we believe in a perfectionist sanctification. What would it mean to be a Free Will Baptist? I mean, how do you make sense of something about free will as crucial to what it means to be a Christian?

So denominationalism, among mainstream Protestantism, is clearly no longer the determinative reality. Therefore, you get Protestantism and Catholicism, and the ambiguity among Protestants to know what it is to be Protestant makes it hard to know what it means to be Catholic since Catholic meant we're not Protestant. So I think how you do theology in such a situation is you try to write for the coming great church—the church that will be born from these climaxes of Protestant Reformation.

Another way that I put it is I think that the Protestant Reformation is over. On the whole, we won. That is, Catholicism is now what Luther would have liked it to have been. I mean, you've got all kinds of bureaucratic issues still involved in terms of what it means to be Catholic. But it means that at least in the world we find ourselves, we are all congregationalists now. I don't like being a congregationalist because I believe in the church universal, and the importance of interconnectedness, so you simply look for a church that can sustain its local parish, and that's the best you can do. But you write for a church that is going to be born from this agony, to be catholic. That's how I understand the ambiguity of, at least my, ecclesial status. Sam's got more of a problem because he's ordained in a very specific tradition.

SW: So I think I understand church in roughly three senses. It is the place where God and time meet—the living example of witness of the incarnation, fully human and fully divine. It is one of the meanings of the body of Christ, just as the Eucharist and Jesus are among the meanings of the body of Christ. Secondly, it is a community of people with all their shortcomings and failings, striving to live an ideal, and forgive, and live heaven now, praying on earth as it is in heaven. And thirdly, it's all the accoutrements related to institutions, involving synods and conventions and money sent from one congregation to a central body, and bishops, World Council of Churches, all of that.

I don't hear a lot of people talking about the first. I guess if it was, it's taken for granted. And the third is seriously out of fashion, although that's where most of the fights are taking place, which gives the fights kind of a sense of irrelevance because they're happening in, to use Neville Chamberlain's phrase, a faraway land of which we know nothing.

So on a personal level, I've grown up in the Church of England and that means I believe that number two and number three have an unbreakable commitment to be a blessing and to receive blessings from the whole population—either in the case of number two, of the parish, meaning the geographical parish, or in the case of number three, the nation, in this case England.

So even if for different reasons one and three are both unfashionable in our era, you can't have a sense of church without all three of those in the end. I think it's either self-indulgent or impoverishing to do so. Number two is the entry point for most people. I guess there are still people who believe in number one who don't participate in two and three. I just don't know what that really means. I guess that's what Stanley was criticizing when he said, in one of his more quoted remarks, that there is no church other than the one with parking lots and potluck dinners.

SH: How do these ecclesial issues relate to discussions about gay participation in the church today?

SW: To the extent that conservatives treat the issue theologically, which is not always to be taken for granted, but to the extent they do, they think they're talking to the first century and progressives tend to think they're talking to now and the next generation or two. In terms of that threefold distinction that I gave, I think the conversation has obviously been significantly around number three: how can a denomination hold together?

Whereas churches where people have changed their mind for number two reasons—either because parents have made a journey that they still love their son or daughter, and the love of their daughter and son has over time become more important to them than whatever they thought were core convictions about sexuality and its expression—all of that has taken place on a more communal level. So two is where change happens.

Part of my own work in that area has been to say we really have to treat this as a number one issue. This isn't an administrative, number three local option, turn a blind eye, if you don't like it you can go somewhere up the road. Again, for a Church of England vicar or rector, that's only ever going to be an interim sort of managerial approach because fundamentally you're committed to making a big tent for your whole community.

And so, in a sense, it should be a no-brainer. If a significant proportion of your community are LGBTQ+ (which they are, deal with it, and if you don't know that you're just not paying attention), then in order to serve your community you need to embrace them unless you have come to the conclusion somehow that it's not possible to be LGBT and Christian, which is a judgment that the church has not made about a soldier and has not made about a usurer. Such people might by historic church doctrine be unacceptable, but they tend to be our biggest donors. So it seems to be inevitable that that logic will extend to say this is a legitimate area of disagreement. You know you could be a pacifist or not a pacifist and still in the big tent; you can be a usurer or not a usurer (although it's hard to find anyone who is not a beneficiary of usury), but these are significant practices that the church has at times in its life excluded and clearly doesn't now.

So to me, the work of ministry is to make a garden out of the plants that you've been given, not to uproot some of them and throw them out. And so, the day-to-day work in ministry is in number two, but the real issues about LGBTQ+ are about creation and eschatology, and therefore they're about the original purpose of God and particularly the final ingathering. If you believe that ultimately God will find a place for all of us then the church's role is to imitate now that final eschatological community. So it's just difficult to see how you can single out one minority within the congregation who uniquely are to be excluded. On what grounds could you possibly justify that, even if you're not yet in the place where you see the blessings this community can give and the way that members of that community can enrich the wider purposes of the church? Even if you can't do that, it's difficult to see how you could justify excluding a group without any regard for their individual gifts.

All the efforts are being made trying to resolve it on a number three level. But for me, those will only be able to do so much good or harm. The issues have got to be worked out on the ground on the two level and they've got to be worked out theologically on the number one level.

SH: The reason I asked Sam about the ecclesial context is because interestingly enough most of the arguments aren't at an ecclesial level. They assume that you can determine issues of gay participation and gay marriage in terms of the presumptions about marriage *qua* marriage, or sexuality *qua* sexuality, in a way that the church doesn't exist. And I think putting it in the ecclesial context is exactly the right way to do it. I'm still unsure of what it does to how you understand marriage if marriage is at least a promissory note for bringing new life into the world.

SW: Well, it changes that. Strong advocates of gay marriage would say but it's perfectly possible today for either lesbian or male gay couples to have children. And, of course, that's true. But I think it presupposes sort of sociological conditions that suggest, for example, that the church in Congo, which doesn't have a lot of access to such possibilities, is irrelevant. It's making what are very exceptional circumstances of IVF and surrogacy and various other routes, normalizing them as opposed to treating them as exceptions. And that's not just changing marriage, that's changing birth it seems to me, from being exceptions to being part of the norm.

So yes, my not original by any means, but my traditional church understanding of marriage, that it's about the turning of the potentially destructive power of lust into a life-giving bonding force (number one), that it's a fundamental, perhaps definitive embodiment of companionship (number two), and that it's the creation of a safe place in which to raise children and accompany vulnerable people (parents, for example, in their later years), I think my sense of that, partly under Stanley's influence, has been that number three is the biggest place of those. And gay marriage is changing the dynamic of that, in which number two and number one become the biggest of those, provided of course, one assumes that marriage continues to require monogamy, which is something that hasn't really had serious public discussion but seems important to raise.

If you believe that creating a safe place in which to have children is the primary goal of marriage (of course there are going to be people who wish they could have children but can't, but leaving that aside for a moment because that doesn't deny the purpose of marriage, it just recognizes that the purpose isn't always fulfilled for all sorts of reasons), and teleologically if number three shapes numbers one and two, then the married couple is obliged by the responsibility of having children to maintain a level of companionship and sexual fidelity because teleologically it is the only way to achieve stability for their children. So even when the companionship is thin and the fidelity is under great stress, the motivation and the responsibility to try again or to renew or to sustain is enormous. But take number three away, then why would you sustain one and two in trying circumstances, when there seem other options available? It does on a practical level problematize the sustainability of marriage as a whole if a safe place to raise children ceases to be the most significant. And that doesn't stop when they get to 18 or 21. This isn't being condemning or judgmental I hope, but the breakup of a marriage will affect a 37-year-old child enormously.

SH: Right.

SW: As Stanley would be the first to point out, this hastening to join an institution whose incoherence has been exposed by this new development is full of irony. But it does press on the church and society generally something that nobody seems to want to do, which is to revisit marriage, with a whole host of new circumstances of which gay marriage is only one.

SH: One of the interesting ways to think about it is that the gay demand for marriage may save marriage.

SW: And the irony that those who are most committed to marriage see their enemy as coming from those who want to join the institution.

SH: That is really quite ironic. I think my general position has been shifting in this way. I'm ready to say, if gay people are ready to take on the same kind of promises that non-gay people take on when they get married—lifelong monogamous fidelity is an extraordinary commitment—if gay people are ready to take that on, let's see how it looks in a hundred years. How changes occur in the church most of the time are not planned; they occur. And then you have to learn to receive them down the line, in terms of how it reshapes the church. Women's ordination I take as one of the same kind of developments. What do you think of that, Sam?

SW: I think I'm more or less in the same place. I mean, I think we've got what I see as sort of a twenty-year window, shall we say, in which suddenly monogamy (having been pulverized for a hundred years) is now all the rage. It's a kind of strange plot development in a novel that at this moment of maximum opportunity for monogamy, the conservatives on this issue are so anxious to reject the energies of those who are new converts to monogamy. That just seems to be a strategically bizarre decision if you think the big game is monogamy. If you think heterosexual promiscuity is preferable to gay fidelity, then good luck to you.

In my twenty-eight years of taking marriages, I have taken marriages of people who *weren't* living together, but [it is a] very small percentage. And so to create a sexual ethic that is being practiced by, shall we say, three or five percent of the population is as stupid a thing to do as the Catholics did in 1968: to create a sexual ethic that assumed Catholics weren't going to use conventional means of contraception. In a sense, you're imagining a number one church that has no connection with a number two and number three church. You're positing an ideal that is so far from the practice of honest and decent people.

So although I say this is a complex development because it problematizes the priority of the number three notion of marriage (the safe place to bring up children), that's what it is and that's what's happening.

SH: My problem with that logic is what it does to nonviolence. I mean you could say that most Christians continue to believe that when push comes to shove you need to kill someone in the name of a nation-state, so get with the program.

SW: Well, the difference I think is that we're still talking about marriage as a good, as a blessing to its participants, but also to their wider community as a way in which God blesses the creation of the church and inaugurates the kingdom. To use my language, if *with* is the fundamental purpose of creation and incarnation and eschatology, then marriage at its best is the most tangible form of *with* that humans have access to. No one's saying that killing is a good. Do you see what I'm saying?

SH: I do.

SW: I mean, I appreciate the force of the argument but that's how I would respond to it.

SH: On the whole, scripture is much clearer on the violence/nonviolence issues than it is on marriage.

SW: Violence and Christian response to violence are at the heart of the gospel, it seems to me. So the question is, are procreative and committed intimate physical relationships at the heart of the gospel? And I think for a Constantinian church, to use a Stanley expression, they have always been. But for a pilgrim church, shall we say (I'm trying to think of a positive word that's not non-Constantinian), are they actually? If we're living with the prospect of the eschaton, any resort to violence is not trusting God's way

of bringing salvation. But you could say any more or less permanent human relationships that were about guaranteeing stability
and order that were not open to the coming kingdom were putting your riches in the wrong place. And that's something that
Stanley has said very articulately in a number of different places,
but I didn't hear anybody else saying that.

SH: If you are in a church that is non-Constantinian, I don't think
you will ever get freedom from the fascination with sexual con-
duct unless you've got other more interesting challenges in front
of you. So when someone comes and says, "Well, I don't understand what's wrong with a little screwing around," you're not
going to convince them in any way by saying we Christians don't
do that. You're going to say we don't have time for that.

SW: And that's a teleological argument, which to me is very per-
suasive. There's something complacent and bourgeois about the
lack of urgency that gives you time to look around the room, as it
were. I think that is a great argument. But it only works within a
view that says Jesus came to disrupt and to portray an alternative
society, and we have to spend all our time imagining, praying for,
dwelling in, and working towards that alternative society. But if
you think Jesus came to secure eternal life so that we can concentrate on making stable families, and he also gave us our self-help
guide to control our temper and all those other kind of things,
that argument doesn't count for anything.

SH: What we are suffering from is a lack of examples, it seems to
me. What would this look like? When I say that the local option
is the only option, what I want that to mean is that if the congregation is open to the witnessing of the marriage of gay people,
they are so because the gay couple has gone through the same
kind of disciplinary process that heterosexual couples have gone
through to see if they're going to promise the kind of commitment to one another that Sam is gesturing towards, that is the

church's standard. And then that means that you're ready to witness the marriage because you see the marriage is going to be for the upbuilding of the holiness of the church. If that's not the case, then you don't do it. So the local option is meant to remind concrete congregations of the kind of work they need to do if you're going to have the marriage of gay people, or better, if you're going to have marriage at all.

Because my sense of the matter is that one of the problems is that the church has been in the marriage game in a way that has been far too accommodating to the presumptions of the culture, namely love creates marriage and this kind of thing, in a way that this is going to mean that many people will not want their marriages witnessed in the church. So it would be one of the places that the church finds itself out of sync with the generalized presumptions of the culture. I think that would be a very good thing.

I don't see any problem, for example, if the church might return to arranged marriages. I mean, so-and-so needs to marry so-and-so. I mean the way that we find one another in marriage today is basically arranged. When I taught marriage at Notre Dame I often pointed out to the kids that Notre Dame was where Catholics sent their sons and daughters to meet people that are basically in the same class, under conditions of the illusion of choice.

SW: While I think that was true then, I'm not sure in a day when people's primary way of meeting one another is on the internet, that those things apply in quite the same way. I'm sure sociologists are studying this kind of thing all the time, but I notice it pastorally—the complexity of becoming quite intimate quite quickly with someone you've met on the internet, compared to the Notre Dame scenario. Because whether or not you call that arranged marriage, you wanted your kid to go to Notre Dame because there were a number of assumptions you could make about the other kids that went to Notre Dame. So if they ended up marrying one of those, it's probably fine. Whereas, the person you met on the internet, you've got no knowledge that anything they told you about themselves is true.

SH: And they're oftentimes not sure that what they tell you about themselves is true.

SW: Exactly.

SH: Do you counsel people that come to you to be married?

SW: Yes.

SH: How many times?

SW: Twice. Once we talk about marriage, and I usually give them the sermon I preached at John and Ana's wedding, if you remember that?

SH: Yes.

SW: And then the second time we go through the service itself. And we talk about words like cherish and—

SH: Do you sometimes say no?

SW: No. As a Church of England priest, I don't have the right to say no.

SH: You're not allowed to say no?

SW: I can say no if they are previously married or don't meet all the criteria, because then they get through on an exceptional criterion, which are of the parish priest's discretion, but I don't have the right to say no to people who live in my parish who are eligible.

SH: You're a civil servant?

SW: I wouldn't say that. I could say I'm not going to take it; you need to ask somebody else. But I can't say you can't be married, because historically when there weren't registry offices, that was the only way they could get married. I've certainly had experiences in preparing people for marriage where I thought, *Really?* Or when people haven't been able to answer a question that I thought was a reasonable question to ask, and I've sat in silence for a minute or two while they couldn't answer it. You know a question like, "Having experienced such a painful breakdown of a previous relationship, what is it about this relationship that gives you such confidence that you want to go ahead with marriage?" And then they're sitting in silence for at least a minute until the partner answered the question for the person who couldn't answer it.

SH: In America, you know, the minister is a civil servant. They have to sign the license of the state.

SW: I do that. And they're not married until I do. I would be quite happy about taking the legal side of marriage out of the church and simply having prayers.

SH: Isn't it true that weddings now cost like $20,000-$30,000?

SW: When I've said, you and Dave have been together ten years, have you thought about marriage? Often the answer is, we can't afford it. It's never the whole answer, but it's often part of it. And in the developing world, rites of passage like funerals and weddings are the biggest single thing that impoverish people apart from illness, because of the obligation to invite the whole community and spend a fortune that you don't have. And part of that's good. I mean, one thing that does keep couples together is the fact that they had a hundred and fifty people at a service, and maybe only three weeks ago. And it's humiliating to say we couldn't sustain that.

SH: When I was at Notre Dame, and because I was a Protestant, sometimes kids would come to me to say, "Well what's wrong with sleeping together?" and I learned to say, "I don't have any objections as long as you have a common bank account."

Conversation Ten

The University / Necessary Conflicts / Decent Human Beings /
Training to Be Eloquent

MKL: We've talked a good deal about the church, but obviously the university has also been a large part of both of your lives. Sam, I don't know if you'd say a lesser degree?

SW: Oh yes, a much lesser degree for me. I've never been sure if I belonged to a university, but Duke wasn't like anything I'd experienced before. It was a joy. The calling to Duke was to Duke Chapel, and it was lovely to have the Divinity School because what's not to like to be a professor? But you see, I'd been a professor without ever having been an assistant or an associate. I hadn't had to do the hard yards of working my way up. And also I went in as a senior administrator at the university who reported to the president and got in on all sorts of conversations I had no right to be on, which for the first couple of years I couldn't understand a word of because they were all about a culture that I had no experience in, the vast department of student affairs, doing jobs that simply didn't exist in my undergraduate university.

So the privilege of that, in many ways completely unqualified and hugely trusted, and I did some stupid things because I didn't have any experience in what I was doing, but I haven't found leaving that a source of grief. The grief about leaving Duke was

127

leaving a role that was a good fit in and leaving individuals and leaving a culture of the university at its best, as a conversation that we talked about earlier. I'd never experienced flourishing in the way that it was during my time here. So to walk away from all that was difficult, but walking away from the university understood as a place where people do research and teach students, that wasn't difficult at all.

MKL: Which is a different answer than you would—

SH: Oh, I'm much more a citizen of the university than I am of the church. The university has been my home since I was eighteen. I went straight through college, straight through seminary for three years, and straight through the PhD. So there was never any break. And then I was lucky enough to get the job at Augustana for two years, and then fourteen years at Notre Dame and over thirty-five at Duke. So it's all I've known. And I of course love the university, and I love what its mission is, which I take to be the formation of students in the wisdom of the culture we call Western and how that reaches out to other cultures. And therefore, I'm deeply committed to what I understand the university is to be about.

I worry whether we're going to continue to be about that. The role of the humanities is under constant stress in the university and I don't want to juxtapose the development of the sciences in relationship to the humanities. Mathematics, I think, is one of the great humanistic disciplines, but I worry that we no longer live in a culture that has sufficient judgments in common that support a university's necessary introduction of conflict into the ongoing understanding of what matters. When you live in a world in which some people think you can't read *Macbeth* because it's denigrating of women, and some people think you can't read *Macbeth* because there are no good witches, and some people think you can't read *The Wizard of Oz* because it's mythological in terms of the fairy godmother and all that, how do you have agreements and judgments about what is significant? The university is a place where that is supposed to happen, where we have the conflicts a culture should have. And I worry that that is being increasingly lost.

MKL: You say in *Living Gently* that "universities are not a means to peace but one of the forms peace takes—they are peace because they explore nonviolently the conflicts we need to have in order to discover goods in common." What are the conflicts the university needs to explore today?

SH: I think one of the conflicts is how is Christianity to be presented in a manner that you are able to know enough about what makes Christianity Christianity to be able to understand a Shakespearean play. That you think you can teach Shakespeare without talking about Christianity is absolutely crazy. That how you present the role of history for an understanding of where we are today I think is filled with conflict, in terms of how you understand the Enlightenment, what it was about and so on. These are conflicts that are necessary for the introduction of students into the world in which they find themselves.

I think that not every student perhaps needs to read Plato, but it's not a bad idea. I think there should be a seminar in the freshman year in which students read *The Republic*. I think there should be a seminar in the senior year in which students read *The Republic*, where they have some sense of the fundamental challenges of what it means to be in a society that should care about justice. The problem today is given the money that it takes to come to these universities, we think that students are no longer students; they're customers and they get to determine kind of what it is they study. You have to submit yourself to the authority of the people representing disciplines that should tell you what it is that you need to study.

It's interesting that if a student is in a physics course and raises their hand and says, "I'm just not sure about electrons anymore," the physicists will say, "Go to the Divinity School." If a student is in a course that says, "I'm not sure about these Emily Dickinson poems. They seem like a frustrated woman to me." They need to be told, "Suck it up, kid. You don't know enough to know what Dickinson was about," just the way the physicist says about electrons. I mean, how to re-establish the authority of disciplinary formation, I think, is extremely important. I don't know if Oxford and Cambridge is going through these kinds of same struggles that we've got in America.

SW: I think the pressures on the universities that don't have the amount of money that a place like Duke does mean they cut corners and ask people to do three jobs, and the research assessment exercise where of course you're writing a book that you have no particular motivation to write but you're simply doing it not because anyone might read it but because it ticks a box for your department, that kind of situation that so many of my contemporaries find themselves in is just so sad.

It's not the case in America. In America you have the entitled tenured professor, which is a phenomenon we don't really have in England, which is a person who exists in a world almost unaware that there should be any reason why, as Stanley put it earlier, being paid to read shouldn't be something that the whole of society wouldn't endorse and exist to make possible. In the UK, you can be a successful academic but you always have that guilty sense that eventually society will catch up with you and expose you for doing something that isn't real. So astonishingly, despite the constant lament about the humanities and the liberal arts curriculum in a university, I look around and think it all seems to be doing mighty fine to me.

SH: I think that one of the challenges is the alienation between the kind of knowledges that are produced in the university and the general American public. Academics write primarily for other academics, and how to write in a way that is accessible to a wider public is one of the great challenges before us. I oftentimes observe that as a theologian I'm way ahead of the game because I have a readership that's obligated to read me. They're called Christians. Of course, that doesn't mean that you're widely read, but it does mean that Christians have a stake in having people who are doing work that is for the critical upbuilding of the church, therefore they need to read it. And they may say you didn't get it right, but that is a very important exchange between the academic and the reading public that on the whole is missing in the university.

Scientists are shaped by power. I mean they do their work funded by the National Science Foundation, the Institute of Medicine, and so on, and therefore they are funded by the presumption by Americans that science is going to ensure the possibility that our lives will be free of illness and even possibly death. That isn't necessarily good for the scientist because the scientist turns out, most of the time, not to be all that concerned about the practical implications of what they're doing. They just love the beauty of what they're about, which I greatly admire. But the American public doesn't get that.

I think my contrast between people going to medical school and people going to divinity school is a good way to suggest in what way divinity schools are also not intellectually serious enough. We [should] expect to train divinity school students at least as seriously as medical school students are trained because having a bad priest is dangerous for your salvation just like having a less than competent physician is dangerous for your health.

SW: I think the analogy in the contemporary church, the last ten years or so, has slightly changed, which is to say those being trained for ministry today I experience as being vigilantly observed about their ability to keep boundaries, respect around sexual power relations, and those kinds of things. The church has got the message, maybe very late, that abuse of power in a general sense has been an epidemic.

So I think the call would be to take the formation in scriptural imagination as seriously as you're taking the concerns about ministerial impropriety of different kinds. There isn't the same rigor attached to the things that Stanley rightly talks about, and I think that's reflected in the church.

SH: I think the training of seminarians over the past fifty years has been inherently a reproduction of liberal protestantism, primarily through the way scripture was taught. I mean, I think scripture being determined by fundamentally the historical, critical method failed to produce exactly the phrase, "the scriptural imagination."

MKL: So, let's imagine there's a youth in your parish who is sensing a call to ordained ministry. What should the discernment and formation process entail?

SW: Well, I think I'd challenge the question, to do a sort of Stanley thing, to say the average age of the person training for ministry in the Church of England is now something like thirty-seven or thirty-eight. And so while I hold to Stanley's convictions about authority and the things that you need to know rather than somehow generate experientially, I do think adult education is different from educating twenty-three-year-olds. And so, I think that while you can share Stanley's convictions, that didactic style is much more complex when you've got people who've got hugely more life experience.

But the recognition that these are adults and that they need to be treated as adults has sometimes come with an assumption that they already have the knowledge they need, we just need to give them the opportunity to articulate it, which is actually depriving them of Origen and Tertullian—people that they may not have come across in their previous experience but who've got something important to tell them. And of course, late vocations are not necessarily a bad thing.

SH: No, they're not a bad thing.

SW: They're not the failure of early vocations. They can be a wonderful thing. But you do have to have the humility to say we need to adapt our educational style.

SH: One of the ways of putting the challenge is how do you train someone to be a decent human being? Bottom line is, you need to be a decent human being that has some wisdom about human relations. I mean, you hear Sam making those judgments all the time as a pastor, about human relations that are wise judgments. How do you train someone to know how to do that? Because it doesn't come naturally, it seems to me. I suppose students watch you make judgments, but that's not necessarily to train them to have them.

SW: This is part of the seminary conversation in the UK where the norm has moved in the last twenty years from residential, almost monastic style education, in the other direction. But how has the teaching to be a decent human being stuff historically been done? My college was twenty-five people (in one year it slipped down to nineteen people), and you can't keep secrets in a community like that. You know each other's business, and you know what they're like at breakfast. It does knock the corners off people, and if people are impossible to live with that does affect their path to ordination. Of course, it is a little absurd because you then spend the rest of your ministry living in circumstances that are wholly different to that. However, it's a kind of a refiner's fire, and that's certainly how I experienced it. The bell goes and you all walk downstairs in the morning in silence together and for half an hour before morning prayer you all have breakfast together.

I think the transition to a much cheaper and more sustainable form of formation sacrifices significant elements of formation. And Jo, who knows far more about this stuff and has been involved virtually her whole career in these kind of issues and still sits on the governing bodies of a couple of these institutions, constantly says that people keep changing the subject when it comes up. How are we doing this in a nonresidential setting? No one is prepared to have that conversation because there is only one explanation, which is that it's just not being done.

SH: Another kind of issue that I think could be said is the importance of seminaries being in research universities. I think that we have a peculiar vocation in this context to take on the fundamental intellectual challenges of what it means to be Christian in a way that commands the attention of the university. I think that it is an issue of power, and it's one of the things that I believe we have the responsibility to do in the world in which we find ourselves. So it's not an abandonment of fundamental ecclesial commitments, but it says those commitments mean that as Christians we need to take on the fundamental intellectual challenges that are present in the university. Part of the problem today is it's not that we're denied; we're ignored. And how to reclaim significance is a real challenge for us.

SW: And that requires a much humbler heart and a more flexible disposition than a lot of divinity schools have managed to attain. It can't be done by shouting louder.

SH: No.

SW: It can only be done by example, and by integrating teaching and practice to a degree that becomes admired by the rest of the university. I remember being asked what's the best thing that the university can do for Durham? And I said the best thing the university can do for the town was to be the university, which takes us back to where we began these conversations with the notion of conversation, where Stanley began his remarks about the university in its ideal form. A university should be a place where the interactions across disciplines—again the clue is in the name "university"—cover everything. We've got to listen to all opinions here. You're not going to be polluted by someone who says something that's really wrong. It's exposed as wrong by the emptiness of its presentation, not by the fact that you refuse to give it a hearing.

The university at its best is a place where people from different disciplines can find common goods but also find interesting disagreements. So that's what I meant by the best thing you can do for everyone else is to be yourself—to be a university. Because it goes without saying that this ability to talk across difference and to listen to somebody who's coming from a different point of view and to entertain an opinion that you personally find offensive and yet to listen it out, are things that particularly North American society desperately need more of. And so the fact that they're cultivated at university gives a living example that it can be done.

SH: I think that the public life in America is characterized by extraordinarily ugly language, and I blame that on the university because universities are communities committed to training people to be eloquent. And that's particularly true of divinity school, which should train people to know how to use language well. The church serves the wider society well when it produces people who can preach eloquently. And one of the great political contributions a university can make to the societies in which they find themselves is exactly to train people to be exacting in what they have to say. That's what we as Christians must do, and it's what I think is extremely important for the future.

Conclusion

SW: My caricature of a Stanley essay would be, because two-thirds of them have arisen from an invited address of some kind, they start by saying that the title I've been given is a really stupid title.

SH and MKL: (*laughter*)

SW: And this illustrates how you—whoever they are, taking the risk of alienating 90 percent of the audience—have got this completely wrong because you wouldn't use words like that or ask the question in that way. So the introductory section is saying, this is ridiculous.

MKL: Right. Do you know how many times as I was preparing questions for this conversation, I thought, well, I can't ask them to "define" something. And I certainly don't want to use the word "values"—

SH and SW: (*laughter*)

MKL: —because language matters.

SH: And you can't use the word provocative.

SW: Right. So then, the body of it is, I've actually just read a couple of books that I'm going to tell you about, and you're not going to have heard of them or know why I'm talking about them, but we're going to do this for a while together. So that's sort of section 2. Then there's a sort of crucial section 3 that shows why section 2 is a better answer but shows what neither of those books have got. And then there's a lament at the end that there wasn't enough time to answer the real question.

SH: My characterization of one of Sam's sermons is, I have three things to say about this, and then they come out in a very lovely fashion.

■ ■ ■

Concluding Reflections

While their preferred mode of discourse may differ, Stanley and Sam share the conviction that language matters. Granted, the sheer length of their publication lists would be enough to indicate a fondness for words. At one point during this project we talked about including a bibliography of their combined works, and even though we agreed the list need not to be comprehensive, I still pitied whomever ended up responsible for compiling such information. (Readers may draw their own conclusions concerning the absence of such a list.) Of course, being prolific isn't the same as using language well. Nor does being a good writer necessitate reflection upon the nature of language. But for Stanley and Sam, language matters.

Stanley's hope, expressed in his opening remarks, that this exercise would push them to say more than what he describes as their "stump speeches," points to the power of language. Good conversation helps us discover things we never knew and unveil things we've always known but have never been able to say. I relished the moments throughout our two days of conversation when together we sat in silence, as one of them searched for words to answer a question, slowly responding with precision and care. Given the volume of their published works, it felt like being let in on a secret to hear them say things I had never heard them say before, or when by their own admission, they hadn't realized they thought something until having said it out loud for the first time. And so, for those who have read a good deal of Hauerwas and Wells, I trust the preceding pages offered you more than the stump speeches you have heard before.

And yet, in view of Stanley's concluding exhortation to be eloquent, I also hope readers heard those stump speeches, no matter how familiar they are with them. Certainly, some will be able to recite verbatim Stanley's speech that modernity names the time when you produce people who believe they should have no story except the story they choose when they had no story; others will anticipate Sam's insistence that abundant life means resisting an economy of scarcity. Those stump speeches aren't indications of weariness, but articulations of the work that has been done to be exacting. Said differently, Stanley and Sam have stump speeches because they found words to say what they mean.

As a seminary student, I learned from Stanley that language is performative. Language shapes how we see the world and who we become, such that eloquent speech isn't about rhetorical flourish but the formation of character. If Stanley taught me language is performative, Sam taught me language can be playful. That in our attempts to reframe terms of engagement and be exacting in what we say, the conversation need not end. Rather, as we look for ways to over-accept what has been given, we are free to playfully improvise, trusting God has given us all we need, and that ultimately the conversation doesn't depend upon us anyway.

Now sitting between them years later, listening as they talk about their work, their friendship and fears, I was particularly grateful for the reminder that all of this is about claiming the everyday. While their voice and context differ, their shared project, upon which their friendship was founded and is sustained, aims to show how the gospel makes the everyday possible. This is why, to answer Stanley's initial question, readers ought to give a shit about their personal lives. Sure, curiosity may prompt a desire to look behind closed doors, but for those who take seriously the claims of their stump speeches, the ordinary is nothing short of extraordinary.

As we prepared for these conversations, Sam once joked that I was responsible for making sure he and Stanley didn't end up only talking about baseball. Of course, their shared project is so central to their friendship that baseball could never be the sole topic of conversation. And yet, the nature of their shared project is such that it would be surprising if baseball weren't part of the conversation. Stanley says Christian hope means living into our eschatological hope here and now. We have been given time to listen, forgive, become friends, and yes, play baseball. The church speaks language of faithfulness, not effectiveness or success. Similarly, Sam says the church has not been tasked with saving the world. The most important events have already happened in the life, death, and resurrection of Jesus Christ, giving us the freedom to live lives in anticipation of what is to come—to claim the everyday.

The radical character of the gospel makes it possible for Stanley and Sam to work on a shared project, learn patience, play Texas 42 dominoes, preach good news, read murder mysteries, love what can be taken away, and enjoy conversation with a dear friend.

Maureen Knudsen Langdoc
Eastertide 2020